HOW TO MAKE A FORTUNE

DURING

FUTURE STOCK MARKET

CRASHES

with

Strategic Stock Accumulation

**Learning A New Investment Strategy
To Buy Stocks And Bonds "On Sale"
With A Definite Rules-Based Formula
As The Stock And Bond Markets Decline**

Stephen Perry

course of action in connection herewith, and as to whether such course of action is appropriate or proper based on your own judgment, and that you are capable of understanding and assessing the merits of any course of action that you decide to take. Individuals should carefully research their own investment decisions and seek the advice of a Registered Investment Adviser.

"Wisely and slow; they stumble that run fast"
-William Shakespeare, Romeo and Juliet

Contents

Dedication

Before Brett, Emily, and Alicia reached young adulthood, I knew each one of my children was capable of building their own financial security. This book was created out of the inspiration of first creating a shorter version to help them in some way along that path.

Acknowledgments

I'd like to thank all those whose contributions made this book possible: Laraine Hruby, my Book Construction Project Manager, whose experience and patience helped me cross many publishing hurdles of which I had no idea even existed; Jeanie Lyubelsky, my Content Editor, as her professionalism, personal encouragement, and positive attitude made it all so much easier; Jim Heilman, my very professional web designer, Subrato Deb, my cover designer and a true artist; my mom and late father, for too many reasons to list; my grandmother, Margaret, whose short old-world lectures to me as a child I can still remember as concerning the importance of saving money; Alicia Rucinski, my daughter, who encouraged me to write this book and helped with the original setup of the back-tested tables; Steven W. Johnson, who did a great job on the final formatting of the book; Emily Savanovic, my daughter, for her input regarding the importance of the editing process; and Brett Perry, my son, who helped inspire me to write this book. This inspiration was borne of the admiration of a father for his son who put college on hold for seven years to serve his country as a U.S. Army infantryman, which included two combat tours in Afghanistan while being awarded a Bronze Star Medal and a Commendation Medal for Valor.

Preface

This book took a while to write—roughly two and a half to three years; however, the investment strategy itself did not take that long to develop. The entire length of writing time was necessary to fully explain and document the strategy's validity in the larger context of the stock market and the entire free-market capitalist system in which investors operate. The 42 detailed tables and 9 charts alone required over 300 hours to complete, and they were completed with no quantitative software or financial programs. All the numbers were individually hand-calculated, checked, and rechecked, line by line, table by table, in a methodical and precise manner. The numbers are correct and reliable; they document and clearly support the positive results of practicing my strategy.

I was on a mission—a mission to explain the truth and offer an explicit explanation of how to make a lot of money during a stock market crash or a severe correction (overall market decline). I expected skepticism. I am not a writer by livelihood and definitely not by inclination. But still, I had developed a passion for communicating this truth. How else to explain sitting down at my computer keyboard hour after hour, day after day, month after month, while other demands of life unsuccessfully competed for time; demands which were routinely ignored, phone calls frequently not made or returned, and exercise that was no longer a regular routine. Extended family and friends, unfortunately, were out of sight and mind. I am not unique in experiencing this personal conflict, I know. No one should (or does, I'm sure) feel sorry for me.

After the crash of 2007–2009, I had developed the basic framework of how this strategy should work. My personal results in that crash are explained in Chapter 1, and it was those results that provided the genesis for this strategy's framework. As I continued to think about it, the development of the specific steps of Strategic Stock Accumulation (SSA) was finally completed by 2012.

Altogether, it was another challenge to communicate clearly on paper as to how such an alien financial idea can be so successful; an idea that demands buying stock as the market continues to drop, even when it drops as far as 50% or more down! Some would erroneously think that this is insanity.

I believe that you will find the explanation of my strategy easy to read. Not only does it make sense, but hopefully my book will stimulate enthusiasm for this strategy that will lead investors to put the strategy into action for realizing its true potential and practical value.

Strategic Stock Accumulation, SSA, is a strategy system that any investor can follow. But just as important, it is a strategy that allows investors to conquer a most feared action of the stock market; an action that takes place, on average, once every four years: the regular occurrence of stock market crashes and severe corrections. The SSA Strategy will result in large profits, with less risk, from exactly those two occurrences.

But how can this be possible without attempting to "time the market"? Accurately determining when to get in and when to get out, or exactly when to buy and sell, is a skill that many "experts" say cannot be done. Many of these same experts also say, tongue in cheek, that it's important to "buy low and sell high," knowing that they can't even do this consistently themselves. They then proceed to tell investors, in one way or another, how they will help them to do exactly what they have just said cannot be done.

But, how is it possible to buy low and sell high if an investor cannot time the market? How is it possible to make a profit without buying in at lower stock market levels and then selling out at higher levels?

I could start to see clearly that there <u>was</u> a strategy in accomplishing this goal, without timing the market. A strategy that would dictate buying and selling regardless of whether the investor thought that the stock market would go up or down in the next few days or weeks. That strategy is Strategic Stock Accumulation (SSA), and this is the subject of this book.

There is a known stock market investment strategy (Dollar Cost Averaging) that emphasizes buying roughly the same dollar amount of stock in bear (trending downward) markets as well as well as bull (trending upward) markets. There is another investment strategy (Value Averaging) that involves investing in down and up markets based on a specific formula. This strategy offers a method of guessing what a long-term market return will be, and then based on that return, calculates a monthly investment amount that should give a desired result by retirement time. There is another commonly used strategy today that rebalances an asset allocation regularly (Asset Allocation and Rebalancing), attempting, in the process, to gain large (largely unsuccessful) profits by buying low and selling high.

Parts or some combination of the above partial bear market strategies are used by many investors. But, to my knowledge, there are no strategies out there that have systematized a valid investment process that invests only in stock market corrections and crashes. Strategic Stock Accumulation is totally unique in this regard.

I saw that it was indeed important to write down and systematize the strategy so that anyone could understand it and put it into practice.

It was even more important to be able to prove that it works. What difference does it make if investors understand how an investment strategy works and can be implemented, if there is no documentation or proof that it will be successful?

Affirmative documentation was indeed accomplished by back-testing three different strategies (including SSA) through six different time periods, going back as far as 1929 (see more details in Chapter 9). The other two strategies tested (and compared with SSA) were two of the most commonly used strategies today, Proportional Rebalancing and maintaining a 100% All-Stock portfolio. I reproduced, as closely as possible, the economic conditions present during those six time periods. I then introduced all three strategies (two of them with three different stock/bond-cash ratios) into those economic environments and watched closely, documenting exactly how they performed. The results are all included in Tables 1A-G to 6A-G, digitally available for viewing and/or print out, and in Chart 9 at the end of Chapter 9.

Strategic Stock Accumulation was easily the most successful of all three strategies back-tested over a 41-consecutive-year period. There is no question in my mind that you will be able see and understand this clearly after seeing these results for yourself.

You will be able to profit greatly from Strategic Stock Accumulation Strategy as explained in this book. Read it. After reading it, you must put the strategy into action!

CHAPTER 1: Why You Should Read This Book

The concept for this book started with a desire to explain, as simply as possible, an investment strategy that my children could follow through their working years and into retirement. Their career paths, academically and professionally, as is often the case, included little or no financial management information or exposure. I wanted to write down some simple rules that they could use, which I learned over 40 years of personal investment experience. I believed that if these rules were followed, they could retire financially secure, regardless of annual income from their respective careers. I retired with that result, and would have done considerably better had I not made a lot of early mistakes that I wanted my kids to avoid. Very soon, I realized that others could also benefit from these rules, if only they were followed. I have tried to explain the strategy in such a way that is understandable to the stock market novice, without boring the seasoned professional investor. Both of these investor categories (as well as almost anyone in between) will realize that a systematic approach to stock market success is clearly laid out in these pages.

How did the ideas for this strategy come about? Why haven't they been written or talked about, especially in the financial media? I don't know the exact answers to these two questions, but I suspect they include a baseless fear of "throwing good money after bad," since the strategy is based largely on a system of buying stock "on sale." That is, buying stock as the market declines. How the SSA (Strategic Stock Accumulation) strategy could be mistakenly perceived this way (throwing good money after bad) will be covered fully in the next chapters.

After my experience in the stock market between 2007 and 2009, the truth of the strategy did become obvious to me. Back-tracking to October, 1987, prior to Black Monday, I was 100% invested in money market funds. Black Monday refers to Monday, October 19, 1987, when stock markets around the world crashed, shedding large amounts of stock value very quickly. The crash started in Hong Kong and then spread to the rest of the world. The Dow Jones Industrial Average had dropped to 1739 and lost 508 points in one day! At that time, I was following a disciplined strategy that emphasized "Don't fight the Fed" and "Don't fight the Tape." Since the Fed was raising interest rates, and the tape ("the Dow") was showing signs of changing direction (downward), I decided not to fight either and went to cash. As a result, I made out very well, buying stock in the next few days, as the market started to come back. I'll talk more about "the Fed" and "the Tape" later in the book.

I lost my focus in 2000, and was "burned" in that crash, which started in the spring of that year, by being 100% invested in stock. I got caught up in the "Irrational Exuberance" of the time and neglected to maintain a sufficient cash position. I didn't sell, however, as the market continued to drop, and I eventually gained back everything that I had lost in that crash, as the stock market retraced back up to its previous high. After being made whole again (that is, back to even), I decided not to put everything that I had into the stock market. Instead, I went to roughly a half-stock, half-cash portfolio.

The financial crisis of 2007 started in the fall. As the stock market then declined through all of 2008 and continued to fall until the spring of 2009, the S&P 500 was ultimately down close to 45%. This time, starting with a large cash position in my portfolio and not knowing how far the decline would go, I started to buy more stock slowly at the end of 2007. I continued to buy stock all through 2008 and into the spring of 2009. By March of 2009, I had no more cash left in my portfolio. I had used it all up, buying stock index funds, as the market had continued to drop. I was now 100% invested in the stock market. This was not my intention prior to the crash; however, I did realize that by the spring of 2009, I had bought a lot of stock at lower prices.

As luck would have it, the stock market stopped its decline in the spring of 2009. So, now I had bought a lot of stock (about 50% of my portfolio in 2007) at below market prices and then watched as the market rose back up to pre-crash levels. This time, I was made whole (back to even) in a much shorter period of time, as compared to the crash of 2000. At some point in 2012, I was up about 150% of my 2009 portfolio value. Of course, many others who had not "sold out" near the bottom were eventually back to even. But, I doubt that many had experienced the large returns that I did, in percentage terms, within just three years from the spring of 2009.

After this experience, I thought to myself, was this just luck? Or was there some pattern that I could take advantage of in the future? Was the stock market likely to react the same way during the next correction or crash, or would it stay down longer than I could, or was willing to wait? These questions fascinated me, and they were the basis for the back-testing research I did in comparing different stock investing strategies, going all the way back to 1929.

I tested three different strategies through both good times and bad, from 1929 to 2013 (not all-inclusive). I wanted to see how the strategy that I was devising in my head stood up against two other common investment approaches. I tested them through five severe stock market corrections or crashes and through six different time periods. The back-testing method I used is clearly laid out in charts and tables and is explained in detail in Chapter 9.

As I thought more about the rules that I had developed for my strategy, I realized that I needed to cover more information about basic investment knowledge. I needed to explain in more detail why this investment process works, as well as how it works within the larger context of our free-market, capitalist economy. Hopefully, this background information will make the investment process more interesting to the novice and experienced investor alike. I've always been interested in political theory, as well as economics. Politics and economics do influence the stock market and have from the beginning of our nation's relatively short history. Many stock market investors, I'm sure, already possess this type of knowledge. Others may find my ideas interesting but not relevant to their purpose in buying this book. If the investor reading this book falls into either of the above categories, please bear with me.

The SSA (Strategic Stock Accumulation) strategy itself includes no political (but a definite economic) philosophy. The rules of SSA include both buying and selling in a strategic manner, the basis of which I have not heard of anecdotally or previously read about in casual or serious reading over a 40+ year period, nor did I find any mention of such a strategy in any research that I did for this book. I believe that my strategy is totally unique.

What is my background, in terms of both education and experience? I graduated from Indiana University with a Bachelor of Science degree in Business Administration, which included courses in finance, accounting, marketing, and economics. During summer vacations while in college, I had gained experience working as a real estate salesman, primarily on listings for a local real estate firm. After graduating from college, I worked as a supervisor in the Remittance Banking division of one of the large banks in Chicago for a year and a half.

I decided not to make banking my career, made a 180 degree change, and entered what is today known as the National University of Health Sciences, formerly the National College of Chiropractic. After considerable health care research, I realized that this natural, drugless, non-surgical approach made a lot of sense to me. Graduation was in 1977 with degrees in Human Anatomy (B.S.), and a Doctor of Chiropractic degree (D.C.). Always being very involved in 'contact' athletics through high school and college, I knew that the more 'physical' approach of chiropractic would be 'natural' for me, and I have since been a practicing chiropractor for 35 years. During that time, I had completed hundreds of post-graduate hours in Chiropractic Orthopedics.

I am now retired. At one time, I owned, and partially managed, 45 apartment units. I traded commodities (corn, soybeans, and U.S. bonds) part-time on the Mid-America Commodity Exchange located in the Chicago Board of Trade Building. I've been an active investor in the stock market continually from my early 20s until now—and I'm 65 at the time of publishing this book.

I still read constantly about markets, economics, and world politics, as well as world economic history. I believe that the more an investor knows about history, especially economic history, the better prepared he or she will be for investing in the stock market, because this knowledge helps him or her to follow an investment strategy with more confidence. The investor is less likely to abandon a good strategy if he or she understands the historical "big picture." One example: knowledge of the "Great Depression" in the 1930s goes a long way toward giving an investor confidence in the knowledge that the market always "bounces back" eventually. I found out through the back-testing process that it came back a lot sooner than most people thought, especially when dividends and deflation are taken into account.

The fear after a market decline among many inexperienced investors is that it will not come back sufficiently in their lifetime to make any future stock market investment worthwhile. They suffer from the investment disease of "*recency.*" This investment malady causes many to experience both greed and fear at different times. They experience greed when the market is in full-blown "bull market" mode (continually makes new highs) and fear when the market does the opposite and goes into "bear market" mode (continually makes lower lows, usually during a recession). What causes these emotional responses to what has always been normal stock market behavior? It is the feeling that what has happened in the recent past will continue to occur into the indefinite future, which is clearly a result of the recency effect.

Recency involves the belief that if the stock market has increased in market value within the last four to five years, it will continue this way indefinitely. The idea is that something has changed in the economy to allow this stock market direction to continue going much higher, for example, than it has in the past. Maybe the change involves high-tech advances or new sources of energy (e.g., oil fracking). The belief is that the upward direction is because of this "something"; therefore, "this time it's different" (four very dangerous words). The investor says to himself: "I'm making a lot of money and all I have to do is "'stay the course,'" and then maybe the "sky's the limit." Or, "I'm pretty sure I'll be able to get out before the market starts dropping again. I'll just sell everything, and I'll already be out at the first sign of a crash."

The different ways of rationalizing belief in the continued upward march of the stock market are legion. This is brought on not only because of high-tech advances and newly found unlimited natural gas and oil resources from fracking technology, but also by offerings such as zero-interest rates to infinity, "The 'Fed' has our back," and more—take your pick. This is the greed factor. We don't want to stop a good thing. The problem is that when it becomes apparent to you that the market has stopped going up and may actually be starting to "crack," it is also apparent, at the same time, to most other investors. Then there is a situation similar to everyone trying to get out of a burning building at the same time. All of a sudden there are very few buyers, many more sellers, and the new bear market begins, sometimes with a slower, but relentless downward drop, and sometimes with a more sudden crash.

Now fear sets in. The investor who just last week, or last month, was up 50–100% or more in the stock market over the last three or four years is now losing 2–5% per day, but he still "hangs on" in the hope of a reversal, which doesn't come. He can't sleep. He kicks himself for not selling out sooner, before the correction or crash started. He's depressed. What he felt before as super-confidence and well-being has turned to fear and loathing (despair). He wishes, above all else, that he still had what is now lost (in his mind).

So now he finally panics and decides to sell out, right at or near the bottom of where the crash has taken the market. When the stock market eventually retraces back up, that money is lost forever, since he has sold out of the stock market near the bottom and cannot regain what he has lost. Why does he sell? Again, because he falls victim to the emotion of fear, and also, to the belief in recency. He thinks that just because the market has dropped 50% and he's lost all of the profits he had made in the stock market, that it will continue to drop, and he will lose almost everything he had to begin with. He thinks that the recent behavior of the stock market will continue indefinitely.

He vows never to go into the market again, because he now knows "it's rigged against the little guy," or "controlled by the Hedge Funds, Big Banks, Speculators, Wall Street"— take your pick. Human failure always needs a "fall guy," someone to blame, someone whose fault it all has to be— and "it can't be me, right?" Wrong! "We have seen the enemy and he is us," as the comic character Linus says. If this investor, and there are tens of thousands like him, had not fallen prey to the emotion of greed, he would have been a lot less likely to have fallen victim to the emotion of fear. How can he avoid this trap in the future? That is, assuming he is willing to accept responsibility for his own investment decisions and invests in the stock market on its own terms. Covering these topics is also an important part of this book.

I will explain a method that is almost failure-proof, if you are willing to accept the stock market on its own terms. I say "almost," because nothing in life is guaranteed. If you are holding four of a kind in a poker game, let's say kings, you can still lose, right? But aren't the odds really, really good that you will win the hand, and shouldn't you raise the ante at that point? You get the idea! Nothing is guaranteed 100%, but this system, Strategic Stock Accumulation (SSA), comes pretty close.

Let's look at the foundation, over and above an

investor's personal investment skill, upon which anyone's success in the stock market is built: free-market capitalism. Why? Because hopefully, this knowledge will start to give you the confidence to not "sell out at the bottom," like the investor I just described. Maintaining this confidence in a declining market is of paramount importance. Even if the SSA Strategy is completely understood and successfully implemented, if the investor subsequently loses confidence and sells out due to fear, then all of this knowledge means nothing.

If you understand how free markets work and how capitalism works, then you will know and understand why the stock market always comes back. This should give you the confidence you need to not sell during a market crash. And, more important, this understanding will give you the confidence to buy during a market crash. So, let's break it down by describing a simple definition of free markets first and then capitalism.

By the way, free-market capitalism can only thrive in a true democracy. This fact is a given. The economies of China and Russia are basically a hybrid of state capitalism and private capitalism. Russia represents this type of hybrid to a lesser extent, than China. But, many believe Russia did simply steal one of the largest oil companies in that country from its private owners. How can we say this type of financial confiscation cannot occur at any time within such a non-democratic country. This hybridization means the state owns large parts of the capital (corporations) of the country; neither country is a true democracy. And their stock markets reflect this economic monstrosity. They are unpredictable in the short-term as well as in the long-term. This is because the state can decide at any moment to change its market capital investment course for political or military reasons with no concern for private owners of capital, such as is true in a democracy.

Surprisingly, most people don't really understand either of the terms, "free market" or "capitalism," in spite of the fact that free-market capitalism is almost totally responsible for the superior standard of living that we enjoy today, not only in the United States, but in most Western and some Asian countries. One reason for this is the almost total lack of emphasis on these two subjects within our educational system. Who remembers studying these terms in school?

So, what does "free market" mean? It is an emotional issue among groups, for example, among members of unions and small business or large corporations who argue about the loss or gain of jobs they say results from free trade. It is true that in the short run, jobs are lost to lower-wage countries, as corporations are relentless in their search for low-cost labor worldwide. This lower-cost labor results in increased profits for the corporations and their stockholders (good for you) but also lower costs for consumers at Walmart, Target, for cars, cell and smart phones, large screen TVs, etc. (also good for you). All these goods (and services) contribute to our increased standard of living. Initially and unfortunately, there is a loss of some jobs, mainly for lower-skilled workers; however, improvements in technology, production, and education lead to new jobs that, over time, replace the numbers and percentages of lost old jobs. If this were not true, the unemployment rate would never decrease, and we know that this is not the case.

"Free trade" simply means allowing one country to sell their goods to another country included in a free-trade agreement, without the buying nation slapping a tax on the product, which the consumer of the buying nation must pay. This means a country like China, for example, can sell low-cost clothes produced in their country to the U.S., without the U.S. government adding an additional tax on those clothes, which U.S. consumers would have to pay in the form of higher prices for those products. This is what happens when there are no free-trade agreements. In this case, China then responds by slapping a 20% tax, let's say, on cars sold by Ford Motor Company in China. Even though China practices state capitalism, it is still to our advantage to trade with them (but their stock market has gone nowhere for years).

The Chinese consumer then must pay 10-20% more to buy a car from Ford. This consumer, of course, doesn't like this idea, and as a result, now is much more likely to buy locally made cars or cars from another country with no import tax. Of course this significantly reduces Ford's sales, and therefore Ford stockholders' profits, because the company must reduce the number of cars that it produces, and since it (Ford) is selling fewer cars, the results are seen in layoffs and lost jobs—the very situation that the opponents of free trade say they want to avoid. This truly is erroneous thinking.

The practice of putting import taxes on another country's goods and services is called "protectionism." The stated goal is to protect jobs and markets in the country engaged in this strategy. In other words, if a country could get away with it, it would just love to be able to sell all of its products cheaply to other nations and have its own people buy only from local "home" businesses. This would result in a very profitable "balance of payments" situation for that country, also increasing the value of its own currency.

Of course, the other countries involved in this "bargain" would experience the opposite situation, so they would never go along with this arrangement, short of military-forced compliance. This forced military compliance is exactly what occurs with a "colonialist strategy." Many colonial Western powers of the 19th century, for example, used military power to force much poorer undeveloped countries to sell products to them very cheaply. So, if all countries engaged in protectionism, world trade would decrease to the extent that worldwide economic recession, and even depression, would be the likely result. This is exactly what happened during the Great Depression, starting in 1929 and lasting well into the late 1930s. Protectionism was not the only cause of the Great Depression, but it was a definitely a large contributing factor.

Of course, if you are one of those whose job is lost, whether as a result of free trade or protectionism, it doesn't matter to you which one was the cause. You don't care if your country and the world as a whole gains from free trade. You still lost your job. But, in the grand economic scheme of things, free-trade wins hands down over protectionism. Many more people are helped than are hurt with free trade. The opposite is also true.

Many more are hurt than helped with protectionism. This is because, in a relatively short time, many more jobs will be lost to protectionism than to free trade. Those jobs most likely will not return until some form of free trade is reestablished. And in the long run, more jobs will be created than lost within a free–trade economy. Also, new jobs created by improvements in technology will have a much better chance to thrive in a free-trade environment, because many of those new jobs will involve sales of technologically innovative products to other countries.

Now, what does a country do when it wants to practice free trade itself, but another country that it buys goods from is reluctant to do the same thing, many times for political reasons? Maybe the first country then only partially practices free trade itself. This is unfortunately, a common problem. The course the U.S. government has followed, in most cases, is to use diplomacy and other forms of leverage to convince other countries to play by the rules of free trade. If the U.S. government responds by retaliating with its own strategy of protectionism, then everybody loses. The U.S. itself is not a 100% free-trade nation. It still protects its sugar market, for example, and has given all kinds of tax breaks to agriculture over the years, even to the detriment of other nations wishing to sell those same agricultural products to American consumers. Why does our country allow even this amount of protectionism? That's easy—politics!

So this makes it more difficult for other countries to sell their products on an "even playing field," so to speak, within those markets in our country. As a result, they are tempted to retaliate in kind. World sugar, for example, is priced much lower than U.S. sugar, but other sugar-producing nations cannot sell it here and make a profit. But, relatively speaking, the U.S. does a better job of maintaining free trade status than many other countries. The U.S. has numerous free-trade agreements with other nations, the purpose of which is to avoid these trade wars that are so destructive to everyone. So this is a basic description of free trade, and it is basically what economists mean when they speak of "free markets" between nations.

Now, what is capitalism, and why does it matter for our purposes? Again, making money in the stock market is dependent on a relatively free-market capitalist system. Your basic knowledge of the capitalist economic framework will help you to make buy and sell decisions with greater confidence.

Many people think that capitalism is the opposite of communism, and in a large sense it is. "Communism" basically means, in economic terms, that the means of production are owned and run by the government. Of course, it also includes a significant loss of personal freedom and rights, as history clearly shows. Pure capitalism, on the other hand, is an economic system where all the means of production are owned and controlled privately and are completely out of government hands. In most countries today that have a so-called capitalist system, the government is involved to some extent in the regulation of the private ownership of "capital." In fact, there is no country today that engages in so-called "unfettered capitalism." The United States probably was close to being such a country for a large part of the 19th century, during the time of the so-called "robber barons."

Some men, such as Rockefeller, Vanderbilt, and Carnegie, made vast fortunes in the oil, railroad, and steel industries. They were almost completely unregulated by the federal government. Unions were either nonexistent or just starting to form during this period. Workers had almost no rights. Wages were at a subsistence level, factory accidents were common, and there was no workers' compensation or other such benefits. Most factory employees worked seven days a week under terrible conditions. Life for most common laborers at this time was miserable. You could even say that they virtually were slaves at this time, at least while they were on the factory floor.

As unions gained more power and politicians listened to the increasing numbers of these voters, things began to change. By the 1970s and 80s, the situation had changed almost to the opposite extreme. Unions, with the help of politicians, listened to these voting constituencies. In many cases, politicians, flush with union donations, allowed unions to gain enough leverage to force unrealistic contract agreements. These new contracts allowed salary and other benefits which were unprecedented. The auto industry, by the 1970s, was a perfect example. The U.S. automotive corporations had agreed to pay workers' salary and benefits at such high levels that they were simply uncompetitive with foreign, mainly Japanese, automakers.

The pendulum then began to swing again the other way, to the point where today, a more "happy medium" has been achieved. Reason more or less prevailed, and total benefits for workers have been adjusted to more realistic, competitive levels. The reason it prevailed was economic but hardly altruistic. As a result, U.S. auto companies are again competitive with foreign companies, and their stock has reflected this change.

There are now laws in place to protect worker rights, as well as social "safety nets" protecting society at large. Social Security, Medicare, Unemployment Insurance, and Workers' Compensation are the most well-known. Most communist nations of the past, and the few that exist today, claimed to care most about worker rights, but the sad truth is that personal freedom and living standards have been severely limited in these countries. Also, the almost complete failure of this economic system has meant that the money required for social safety nets in all communist systems has been sorely lacking. Communism also lends itself to a greater risk of corruption within the economy. The lack of personal freedom limits any attempts for popular economic oversight. Of course, democracies with free-market capitalistic economic systems also experience corruption. The difference is that in democracies, the so-called "fourth estate," or the free press, is much more able, and likely, to shine a spotlight on corruption.

If you did not know all of this before, you now have a basic understanding of the terms "free trade" and "capitalism." Don't get lulled into thinking that protecting jobs from going over to foreign countries actually saves jobs. In a relatively short time, this practice actually causes the loss of jobs. Free trade is the only way to go, as most Western nations have figured out. What does free trade and protectionism have to do with the stock market? Everything! Because if politicians succumb to the pressure to "save jobs" by resorting to greater levels of protectionism, this will be bad for the stock market, and not only in the long run. The results of protectionism will soon be reflected in the stock market, because the market always looks ahead and will deduce quickly that the country is becoming less competitive due to the restrictions on foreign competition. This will reduce corporate profits, and stocks will suffer.

Now, having said all of the above, money can still be made in the stock market as a result of a severe stock market correction, regardless of the source. As stock is bought during stock market declines, it will certainly gain value as the market inevitably cycles back up toward its previous high. And, this will <u>always</u> happen in a free-market capitalist democracy.

If the stock market declines to a point where it is undervalued, it will eventually return to fair valuation. This is called "reversion to the mean," which means that it cannot stay undervalued indefinitely and will "revert" (in this case, "revert" means that the market goes back up, not down) back closer to an average (mean) fair value. However, if protectionism is practiced by the government to that extent, the stock market's retracing to its previous high may well be delayed, until government policies change. This is why free markets are so important to the stock market investor.

The bottom line is that free trade is important not only to keep unemployment from remaining at unacceptably high levels, but also to allow the engine of corporate profits, and therefore standards of living, to continue to rise. This will lead to those increased profits being reflected in higher stock prices.

Now I hope that I've convinced you of where your interests lie as a stock market investor, as well as a consumer, in deciding the merits of free trade versus protectionism. Others on both the left and right of the political spectrum may disagree and often do. Disagreeing people and groups are usually either personally or politically motivated with their own agenda. In the big picture, there is no contest between these two economic options. Free-market capitalism is best. By and large, this is our system in the U.S. As long as it is, you can be confident that the stock market will 'always come back' from a stock market crash or correction. So, don't sell at any point during these two "problematic situations."

There is another problem related to free-market capitalism that is important to discuss. It is the argument between legal lobbying and the attempt to characterize all lobbying of government-elected officials as bribery. Let's look at this popular indictment a little closer. It certainly seems to be a logical knee-jerk reaction to believe that the charge of bribery is true. After all, why should an elected legislator who is directly involved in making laws for everyone be influenced at all by financial donations from any lobbying group, whether it is a union or big corporation money? As I said earlier, union lobbying up to the 1970s was instrumental in giving the unions leverage to negotiate salary and benefit agreements that were ultimately so high as to be counterproductive to the auto industry and workers as a whole.

We can go further back in U.S. history to the 1800s, when the large steel, railroad, and oil trusts used their financial power to influence legislators. This resulted in extreme pro-business legislation at the expense of basic worker rights. Even so, it is undeniable that many of the so-called robber barons mentioned earlier were instrumental in the early industrial development of our nation, to the extent that it laid the groundwork for U.S. industrial pre-eminence in the 20th century. This largely contributed to the future rising living standards for all of us. Certainly, worker welfare was largely ignored during this time as a situation that needed to change, which it subsequently did.

So, isn't all such lobbying by left and right wing organizations, if not outright bribery, then at least obviously corrupting our legislative process? Well, the U.S. Supreme Court doesn't think so. How can this be? Can't the highest court in the land see this lobbying money for what it really is—outright bribery? The answer is, "no."

The U.S. Supreme Court has called large monetary donations (within certain legal parameters) to elected officials "protected free speech." In other words, if I have enough money, I can use some of it to influence how I think laws should be passed. In other words, my money is my mouthpiece. It certainly sounds like some people, in following this reasoning, have much larger mouthpieces than others. So is this fair?

I would argue that lobbying by interest groups is necessary, and here's why. First, to put this thinking into proper perspective, let's go back in time to the ancient civilizations of Rome and Greece. Some of you may now be thinking, "Rome and Greece? What the hell is this? I didn't buy this book to get a lesson in ancient history"! Please bear with me. However, if you are in no way interested, skip the next few paragraphs, or better yet, skip the rest of this chapter. I know many investors already have a very good understanding of how free-market capitalism should work in a democracy. If that's the case, no problem; just go on to Chapter 2.

Rome was a republic, not a pure democracy. It was a republic in the sense that laws were passed by the Senate. The Senate was elected by the free male (not slave or female) citizens. This republic lasted approximately 500 years and was arguably a very good form of government at that time. It probably allowed for the greatest amount of freedom possible at that time in history. Then it was destroyed and replaced by an imperial system that lasted another 400 years. This was arguably a very bad form of government. The imperial system was maintained for that long period of time, mainly as a result of Rome's military power as compared to other nations and not due to good governance.

The Roman Republic of the first 500 years was ultimately destroyed as a result of the struggle between the rich Patricians and the common, usually poor, Plebeians. This struggle culminated in the achievement of absolute power by the Roman general, Julius Caesar. He gained power through the voting support not only of the poor masses of Rome, the "plebs," but even more importantly, of the mostly poor and landless military under his command. His ability to also give the spoils of war to his soldiers made them more loyal to him than to the Senate, and therefore, to the government of Rome.

Caesar was ultimately assassinated by members of the Senate who thought they would be hailed as heroes for returning Rome to its republican past. They were mistaken. All the people of Rome remembered was that Caesar had increased the grain dole given freely to all citizens of Rome. Most of these "heroes" who killed Caesar were then forced to flee Rome and a Civil War ensued. Augustus, Caesar's grandnephew, was victorious in that struggle and continued the dictatorial imperial system of Caesar.

This was the end of Rome's Republic and the beginning of its big-government imperial system. It was then subjected to a succession of emperors, many corrupt, who did away with most forms of personal freedom. As Roman freedom decreased and corruption increased (as it always does in a dictatorship), it slowly lost its position as the pre-eminent world power of that era, and it was ultimately overrun and destroyed by different foreign, mainly Germanic tribes. The bottom line here is that the outnumbered "rich" were "outvoted," so to speak, by the masses of the "poor," and everyone in that society suffered as a result.

The ancient Greeks had a more pure form of democracy. All free citizens in Athens, for example, were allowed to vote on all legislation before it was passed. This was not a representative form of government in which legislators, voted in by the people, made the laws of the land. All the people made all the laws by everyone directly voting on everything. The main problem with this system of pure democracy was that it was very slow and cumbersome. There was no way for the upper class to speed things up and protect their private property.

It was this slow pace of governmental action in Greek democracy that doomed it from within. Before any military action could take place, all free citizens, rich and poor, needed to vote for it. So when Alexander the Great (of Macedonia) was marching in on Athens, it took too long for the city government to decide on any military action, because it required weeks or months to logistically accomplish a successful vote. By the time military defense was approved, it was too late. Alexander had moved in to conquer much more quickly than Athens had decided to defend itself. At any rate, Athenian democracy was finished. The equal influence of everyone at all times, rich and not so rich, destroyed it. The rich were not able to use their economic resources to help defend their country. As a result, they and their country lost everything. What does this have to do with lobbying? I'll get to that in a minute.

No pure democracy (which is more like socialism) since then has ever succeeded. No less a liberal than Thomas Jefferson, himself, said, "Democracy is a fraud in which 51% of the people take away the rights of the other 49%." Former British Prime Minister Margaret Thatcher said, "The trouble with socialism (democracy to the extreme) is that eventually the government runs out of rich people to tax." Ronald Reagan said, "We are only one generation away from the loss of freedom." The bottom line is: The defense and protection of our free-market, capitalistic republican (type of government, not political party) form of government, is most important.

So, what does this simple history lesson have to do with present-day lobbying, or even more important, the stock market? A lot! Socialist Europe, and increasingly America, are object lessons. What inevitably happens as time goes by is that those who have little or nothing, and even some considered middle class, continue to confiscate assets from "the rich." How do they do this? Through their elected officials in the form of taxation. As taxes go higher and higher (more and more free grain for the citizens of Rome), the poor are required to do less and less in order to live a comfortable life. Over half of all U.S. adults now do not work!

As assets, in the form of private property (money), are stripped from those that create wealth, they have less and less incentive to create more wealth through private enterprise. Why should they? Most of it will just be taxed away anyway. Eventually this confiscatory taxation destroys a free society, as the rich are forced to give up more and more of their private property in the form of ever-increasing taxes, or what is referred to as their "fair share." I always wonder what is "fair," and who decides this? Certainly not those who are required to pay. This is what has already happened in Europe, mainly the southern part, and exists as the present trend is in this country. As mentioned above, more than 50% of the U.S. adult population does not work. What do you think the majority of these people want their elected officials to do in the way of taxation?

Please don't misunderstand me. I'm not saying that taxation is wrong or unnecessary. We must have taxation. Taxation is important for many reasons, such as the ordering of a civil society. Basic social safety nets—police, fire protection, and national defense, are all dependent on the taxation of citizens. It is <u>excessive</u> taxation on those who create wealth that can be very detrimental to an economy and to the nation as a whole.

Now, having said all of the above, there is a valid argument to be made that in spite of high tax rates, the gulf between the rich and the poor is large and increasing. This is true. This is probably truer today, because the rich were able to take greater advantage of the last four extremely profitable stock market years. This market opportunity increased their personal wealth significantly.

Large parts of the middle and lower U.S. economic classes had little or no money invested in the stock market. In many cases, those who did have money in the stock market were not able to make themselves whole after losing half of what they had in the market and in the value of their homes, as the housing market also dropped drastically. Many voters sold all their stock as the market continued to drop. Big mistake! Many people also lost their jobs and some of them were not able to find new ones comparable in salary to the old ones. Many recent college graduates were and are unable to find jobs that allow them to even begin to make a dent in their college loans. Why does this increasing economic disparity matter, aside from the moral question? It matters economically because the rich don't spend all of their money! They reinvest most of it. The middle class and poor usually spend most, if not all, of their disposable income. That is the major reason that the U.S. economy has been slow to recover from the last recession.

The argument can be made that if there were a more even distribution of money, the middle and lower economic classes would spend more and the economy would respond much faster. If few are spending because most don't have much money to spend, then this slows everything down. This is most likely what has happened.

So, what am I saying now? Are high tax rates, in an effort to redistribute income more evenly, now okay? The U.S. tax code needs to be changed. Corporate taxes should be reduced. They are among the highest of the Western democracies, and this fact simply discourages more investment by corporations operating within this country. The top personal tax rates should be raised—but not excessively, to avoid nearing the level of confiscation. What is excessive? Excessive would be that level of taxation that starts to discourage investment. Don't ask me what number that is. I'm not a tax expert. I do believe economic disparity is dangerous, just as excessive taxation is also dangerous.

When profits are excessively taxed, why take on the risk of investing at all? A balancing act, therefore, is required. It shouldn't be difficult to understand this philosophically or to understand the point at which the tax situation has gone too far in one direction (too high) or the other (not enough). The difficulty is in finding and passing into law a tax code that effectively puts more spending power into the hands of those of us who are most likely to spend—and to do this without excessive taxation.

Let's get back to lobbying and the U.S. Supreme Court. What I am saying, and what the U.S. Supreme Court agrees with, is: The only way private property can be protected from confiscatory taxation is by opposing the influence of the greater voting power of those who would take that property and by influencing legislation to the point of protecting that private property. This can only be accomplished with money—appealing for legislative support and protection through financial donations, which the Supreme Court terms, "free speech." If lobbying was made totally illegal, imagine what would happen. It would only be a matter of time before politicians, with no more lobbying money, realized that they could still get elected (and receive a very good paycheck). They simply need to promise paying more and more (and then force the rich to pay through laws that they pass of their "fair share") and to increase the benefits for everyone else to unrealistic levels. The moral hazard here is obvious. Will people willingly work if they don't really have to? In a very real sense, there would be no way for private property to be protected at all from extreme taxation. And this means that the government (that can give the people everything or can take everything away) ceases to protect, which leads to the end of democracy, goes down the slippery slope to pure socialism, then totalitarianism, and finally, complete economic stagnation.

So as a stock market investor as well as an American citizen (or any citizen of the world, for that matter), it is vitally important to you that our nation continues as a free-market capitalist republic (true democracy). We must be able to control taxation, keeping it at the level of maintenance of an adequate social safety net for all, but not allowing it to rise to near the level of outright confiscation. At the same time, the economic disparity between the rich and everyone else cannot continue to increase without seriously affecting the economy.

Why has the U.S. always been the leader in new technology and innovation? Free, private enterprise, capitalism, supported by protected private property, that's how! The next chapter describes increasing your own private property (stocks, bonds, and cash) through the strategy of "saving money." Possessing the initial capital to invest is obviously important to the strategy of Strategic Stock Accumulation, which will be explained in Chapter 8.

CHAPTER 2: Saving Money

This chapter may be redundant to many investors. When I consider the typical reader of a book like this, I'm probably preaching to a very large choir. Again, if this information does not add to what you already know, then simply go on to the next chapter. At the same time, I have included this topic, because it is vitally important to many people.

Let me emphasize no minimum amount of money is required to use the Strategic Stock Accumulation Strategy. Even a small amount, such as $10,000, could be used as an initial investment. Any amount smaller than $10,000 will pose a problem with some (but not all) brokerage firms. You should be concentrating on saving, as opposed to investing, at this starting point anyway. Ideally, you should begin the SSA Strategy with at least $33,000.

Saving money is one part of successful investing that is just as important as effective stock market investment strategy. This means that you must focus on the steady accumulation of investment capital (money), through the continual habit of saving. I realize that for many readers, this information is well-known and accounted for. But for others, it can be a problem. Unless an investor inherits the money used in wealth creation in the stock market, then it must come from other money set aside over time: money resulting from one's own labor. This is very difficult for many people to do consistently. Why is this the case? It can be because of other more perceived pressing financial obligations. More often than not, however, it is due to the desire of many people for current consumption, as opposed to future security.

It's commonly reported that up to 75% of all people nearing retirement, by their own estimate, will not have enough money to retire at 62, or even 65, at the same standard of living as they had experienced while working. Social Security will no longer be enough for most people. They will simply be forced to work longer or experience a lowered standard of living. Investing in the stock market, except for nominal amounts in a 401(k), or IRA, is not as high of a priority as it should be.

Unfortunately, many humans are not wired for, or educationally capable of, seeing the importance of regular, consistent saving. This is more important than successful stock market investing, because if there is no money, then there is no investing. The importance of regular savings habits can be taught when emphasized from an early age. So many different subjects are taught in school from primary school through college, and yet there is almost nothing taught about one of the most important subjects affecting everyone's future. Almost anything talked about and emphasized early enough in life can settle somewhere in the back of the brain to be called upon at maturity for future use. This is the whole idea behind education.

Why not have a "60s-type space race" kind of effort in this area that is of such national importance. We all know that Social Security is bankrupt. There is no money in the system. Present retirees are simply paid by present workers, through those workers' present salary checks. Even if this system were to be somehow "fixed," it would not be enough for most people to maintain their 'working years' standard of living. You don't have to fall into this trap. It's never too late to start the good habit of saving money. In many cases, it's later than it should be, and in some cases, it's almost too late. In most cases, however, a level of future security can still be salvaged. The sooner people start, the better off they will be with savings and future opportunities.

Even if an investor decided to forgo the stock market completely and invest only in a combination of bonds of different maturities and money market funds, he or she probably would retire much more financially secure, as long as this approach was started soon enough. Whether it's stocks, bonds, or money market funds, the most important first step is to have the money to invest, and for most people, this means saving regularly out of an income stream resulting from their own labor.

So, what is the best way to save? Aside from following a savings system as I'll describe shortly, the best vehicle by far is a 401(k) or IRA-type of tax-sheltered structure. Most people are aware of the tax benefits that an IRA can give to anyone who pays taxes. In a traditional IRA, a tax deduction can be taken on up to $6000 per year, depending on a person's age. The money accumulates tax-free over all the years that it remains in the IRA, until it begins to be withdrawn. At that point, taxes must be paid as the money is taken out. With a Roth IRA, no deduction is given, but the money accumulates tax-free, and no taxes are paid upon withdrawal, assuming that the investor waits until at least age 59 ½. A Roth IRA is preferable to a traditional IRA in most cases. Why not pay the taxes upfront and be secure in the knowledge that they will never need to be paid again?

A 401(k) is treated much the same as a traditional IRA for tax purposes, but usually, more money can be set aside this way based on an employee's salary. A tax deduction is taken upfront, the money accumulates tax-free, and taxes are paid at normal income tax rates as the money is withdrawn during retirement. A big advantage of a 401(k) is that in most cases, the employer participates to some extent, possibly even matching the employees' contributions that are deducted from his or her salary. Always take full advantage of this employer benefit. The Strategic Stock Accumulation Strategy should be used within the tax-free structure of IRAs and 401(k)s, whenever possible. Let these assets accumulate tax-free for as long as possible.

How can we accomplish this consistently, over time, and still pay all of our bills while having enough left over for "enjoying life," however we may define that goal? The best way to do this is nothing new. The idea has been around in print for probably at least 100 years in the US. It is simply, "pay yourself first." This is done by holding money aside before paying any other bills or making any type of elective purchase that is not necessary, even if you think you need it to "enjoy life." Practice consistently, every payday, to pay money into your own savings and investment account before you spend it on anything else, whether it is rent, food, etc. On reading this, some may ask, "isn't it more important to pay for life's necessities before worrying about a savings plan?" I am here to tell you, "no, it isn't!"

You simply must act as if your income is 10-15% less than it is. You can save 10 to 15% in an investment or savings account and budget the remaining 85-90% according to life's daily necessities. We could all live on 85-90% of our present incomes, if we had to, without starving to death or anything closely as tragic. And if we have to go without certain things that we feel are vitally important to the present enjoyment of our lives, well, all I can say is, "it's better to go without them when you are young and strong, than when you are old and weak with little or no retirement savings. Many old and retired people with moderate to severe medical issues wish they had saved a lot more when they were young and could do so. Now, it may be too late for them. What should be the "Golden Years" of retirement ends up as a constant struggle to pay bills and deal with worries of poverty.

Don't fall into the trap of denial and complacency. Some psychologists have said that denial is the most advantageous mental strategy of man, allowing him to survive extreme emotional and physical or potentially deadly situations of life. It allows him to continue functioning until possibly the worst comes sometime in the future. Well, I don't believe in the success of that strategy at all, and neither should you, especially as it regards your actions concerning retirement and every other facet of your life.

It's so easy to stick our heads in the sand and start making excuses. Some people use the "everyone's doing it" or "no one's doing it" reasoning to justify making poor financial decisions, such as:

"There are just no jobs out there!"

"Nobody can afford to buy a house."

"You can't save money with the economy the way it is these days."

"You try putting three kids through college, pay a mortgage, pay for two cars, and then see if you can save money. People just can't do it now!"

It's almost like if we just all stick together in denial, we'll all be alright in the end. No, unfortunately, it doesn't work that way. There have been many cases throughout history where whole societies have experienced utter catastrophe through mass denial.

The average life expectancy is continually going up, and you may live a long time; a lot longer than you think. Don't let those years be in poverty and worry. Some say, "Life is short." It can seem very long if you are worried about paying your bills every day and end up impoverished, at the mercy of some teenager with emotional "issues" assisting you in a nursing home. Yes, bad things like that happen—more often then you may think. My mother worked in a public nursing home for at least 10 years, and I can still remember the horror stories she told concerning the treatment of the residents by some of the "caretakers" working there.

This brings up another issue that is very important. I believe that most people, if they can afford it, should strongly consider buying a long-term health care insurance policy. After health issues begin, it may be too late to get a decent policy, unless you are willing to pay much higher rates than before any medical problems occurred. There are some very good policies available that give the policyholder much more control over their care, including how all benefits will be paid as well as where and how often care can be given. I know it's difficult for many people to think about this. It's just easier to believe that a spouse or family member will "be there" for them when they are no longer able to take care of themselves. Or, they think they may die quickly from a heart attack or stroke and all the premium payments will be wasted. This certainly could happen, but this kind of insurance is for the statistical likelihood that perfect health leading to a quick death will not happen. Most people don't see their houses being burned down, but that doesn't stop them from buying homeowners insurance. It's the same idea with long-term care insurance. Hopefully, it will never be needed. But, what if it is, and then you don't have it? Personally, I don't want to take the chance of having few options, should this situation occur.

Of course, even with a long-term care policy, you could still end up in a nursing home. But at least most, if not all, of the savings and investments that you have accumulated for retirement would not need to be spent on nursing home care. This money could then be enjoyed or left in your estate and directed to whatever ends that you have decided upon, whether it is for your children, spouse, or charitable causes. With no long-term care insurance, nursing home care cannot be covered by Social Security alone. Most of your savings and assets, if not everything that you worked for all of your life, could be used up quickly.

There are some nice features in some of the new long-term care policies. Some allow more options than simply paying for entry and residence in a nursing care facility. One option includes a provision for home care by a caregiver of your choice, if round-the-clock nursing home care is not necessary. This caregiver might, with your agreement, come to your home several days or more each week and be paid out of your policy limits. In some policies, you determine the caregiver and how much he or she would be paid. Also, if the time comes when 24-hour care is needed, a good long-term care policy could pay for a large part, if not all, of private nursing home care. That is certainly what most people would want.

What is the solution then to these old-age challenges? Money! Yes, money! Everyone has heard it said that "money can't buy happiness." Maybe not directly, but lack of enough money for daily living expenses can sure make life miserable. No question about it. So, pay yourself first from now on. One relatively painless way to do this is to have 10–15% taken directly out of your checking account once a month. If you are contributing to a 401(k), then consider this as a part of your total monthly savings. By having money automatically deducted from every paycheck, you will adjust your spending habits accordingly and probably not even miss the saved money. It's all a matter of budgeting accurately with the remaining 85–90%.

We all have to make decisions in life: the decision (if at all possible) to go to college or not, resulting in greater or lesser lifetime income; the decision when and if to get married, to have children (and how many), to take on mortgage debt of a certain size; the decision to pay off a credit card every month or make minimum monthly payments on it instead; the decision concerning overall debt level in relation to income; and finally, the decision involving current elective family consumption habits.

You can see where I'm going with this. Very few people are forced into untenable financial situations that could not have been avoided with some pre-planning and sticking to a budget come hell or high water. The problem in most cases where these methods fail is that spending for current elective consumption, such as alcohol, smoking, eating out frequently in restaurants, overspending on kids, etc., is simply out of control. Then, rather than trying to deal with the problem logically by starting and sticking with a savings program and budget, it's just too easy to go into denial mode.

My goal is to get you to save money, no matter where your life's decisions have put you right now. Then, when you've reached a level of savings that includes a three-to-six-month emergency reserve, you can begin an investment strategy, such as Strategic Stock Accumulation (SSA). As I said before, it's never too late to improve your financial situation, especially in the good ol' U.S.A. I hope that I didn't offend some people with these last remarks, but I am talking now like I would, and have, talked to my own kids. So, it's hard for me to sugarcoat the subject of personal financial decision-making.

What is the best way to approach a debt-reduction program? Many books have been written on the subject, and most of them correctly recommend eliminating smaller short-term debts before tackling the larger ones. This method allows you to more actively see an overall reduction of your total debt. Allocate a certain amount of money each month, just as you do for your savings program, toward debt reduction. If money is tight, an effective strategy could be to allocate 5% to savings and 10% toward reducing non-mortgage debt. Don't count your mortgage payment in your debt-reduction program, until all other debt is paid off first. Then pay extra money on your house mortgage every month. When you are debt-free, you can then allocate 15% toward your savings and investment program from that point onward.

The important subject of saving money should not be discussed without including this subject of eliminating, or at least controlling, debt. Large amounts of debt, relative to income, can be devastating to you and your family's financial future. So, a debt-reduction program should be instituted, as soon as possible, in every situation where debt is a problem. In the same way, simply allowing more money to be used for an investment program as soon as possible will also be helpful.

All or even most debt does not have to be completely eliminated before starting a savings and investment program. As mentioned above, the best way to approach this challenge is to save money and reduce debt at the same time. Why is this so? Wouldn't it be better to get rid of all non-mortgage debt before beginning any investment program? After all, doesn't the interest paid on most debt negate the gains made from savings and investment? Maybe, to some extent... however, as your savings and investments grow, you will be able to see progress not only in reducing debt levels but in actually making definite progress toward financial security in retirement. Don't underestimate the importance of this emotionally positive reinforcement. This will allow you to see your debt decreasing as your assets increase. Your debt will eventually be eliminated if you do this consistently, and your net worth will continue to grow as your assets increase in the form of a larger investment portfolio.

One way to plan the strategy of a savings and debt-reduction program is to begin with a budget that lists all
income and expenses. Then, you can break the expenses
down into three broad categories: 1) necessities of life—
food, shelter, gas, electric, etc., 2) life-maintenance necessities—insurance, car for work, tuition, and clothing, and 3)
elective expenses—travel, restaurants, more expensive
clothing, and other non-necessary elective expenses. Now,
subtract your 15% from your total income and allocate 10%
to debt reduction and 5% to savings, as explained before,
paying the shorter-term debt off first. If you are already
debt-free, then allocate the entire 15% to savings. The
remaining 85% of your income is then allocated to your 3
broad categories of expenses. The more of the elective category (#3) that is eliminated, the better; after subtracting
15% from total income for savings, the first 2 categories
may use up most of the remaining money (i.e., 85%), and
there is little left over for the elective category. On the other
hand, it is certainly possible that expenses can be reduced
somewhat in the food, shelter, and car expense category by
shopping a little wiser.

One simple way to estimate how a beginning investment program will grow is called the "Rule of 72." You
simply divide the number 72 by the expected interest rate
received or return expected on any initial investment. For
example, if an investor starts with $1000 invested in bonds
that pay an interest rate of 5%, then the expected time for
the $1000 to double to $2000 is 14.4 years (72 divided by 5
equals 14.4). I mention this simple formula as a way to
make a "ball park" estimate of your overall investment
return from time to time as you begin an investment program. This simple exercise gives you some practice in
thinking about the possible future returns of your portfolio.
Additionally, it's fun to think about!

To summarize: you should, first of all, set a goal. It
could be to retire with enough money to live on and to
make your "Golden Years" truly golden. It could be to be
able to retire earlier than 65, or even earlier than 62. It
could be to become debt-free and financially independent

by age 55. Whatever it is, write it down, and then break down the steps necessary to achieve your goal. This should include consistently paying yourself first with the percentage of your income that you decide on (hopefully, at least 15%) and then developing a budget, like the one I had described. The next step would be to memorize and follow the stock market investing rules that I will describe in the chapter on "Strategic Stock Accumulation: The Method— Step by Step."

Finally, I would recommend that you follow the tried-and-true approach of Napoleon Hill in his classic work, *Think and Grow Rich*. The most important rule in that book is to read your goals out loud twice daily. Include as part of the goal, the exact method by which you will achieve it, and the time limit to do it. Many others have tweaked his method over the years. His method is the original, and the savings and debt-reduction program as I just described can easily be added to it. Follow it, and add the method of Strategic Stock Accumulation (as explained in its own chapter on "The Method—Step by Step") to the action steps and goals that you need to read daily. If you do this, you will be doing more than 99% of the U.S. population for the planning of your retirement and financial success.

CHAPTER 3: One Necessary Term and Other General Information

I chose the title for this chapter with the idea in mind that a lot of the information covered herein is extraneous to the Strategic Stock Accumulation Strategy. In other words, there is only one term in this chapter necessary for effective implementation of the SSA Strategy. However, the rest of the information covered will definitely be helpful to any investor interested in how the stock market actually works. For those already knowledgeable, this chapter will still serve as a good basic review. At any rate, everyone must know how the P/E-10 ratio is used within the SSA Strategy.

The price/earnings (P/E) ratio is the term necessary for all investors to understand. A variation of it (P/E-10) is included as one of the selling rules of Strategic Stock Accumulation, as covered further in Chapter 8.

Price / Earnings Ratio

You will need to understand and use a variation of the **P/E, or price/earnings ratio**, as part of the SSA

Strategy (that variation will be explained shortly). This really is not difficult. **This ratio measures the relationship between the price of a stock, exchange-traded fund, or the stock market as a whole to the earnings per share of either a stock, ETF (exchange-traded fund), or the market as a whole.** So, if the price per share of stock xyz is $40, and the earnings per share for the last year for xyz is $2, then the P/E ratio is 20 (40 divided by 2 = 20). This, by itself, would indicate probable overvaluation for xyz (the long-term average P/E ratio for the stock market as a whole is 14.5). This is usually calculated to cover the last twelve months and is termed the TTM (trailing twelve months).

Most analysts consider the P/E ratio as a very good way to help determine overall stock market and individual stock valuation. This is because if the earnings of the S&P 500, for example, are increasing, but the overall price level of this index remains at what previously had been considered a fair valuation, then all other things being equal, the stock market is probably becoming undervalued. The same is true for an individual stock, or ETF. If the earnings of an individual stock or index fund continue to increase, then at some point the market will recognize this, and those stocks should increase in price. For the purposes of SSA, we are concerned only with the overall value of the total stock market (using the S&P 500 as the benchmark).

John Maynard Keynes, the 18th century British economist, said, "in the short run, the stock market is a voting machine; in the long run, it is a weighing machine." In other words, in the short run, psychological [sometimes called "animal spirits"] factors can overwhelm the stock market, causing it to move to extremes, up or down, not based on true valuation [voting machine]. Eventually, however, the stock market will revert to fair value [weighing machine]. The P/E ratio is a tool to "weigh" the value of the market.

There are certain caveats to the validity of the P/E yardstick. For example, in a severe market crash, or even a moderate "bear" market, the earnings may decrease much faster than the overall stock price. In this case, the P/E ratio may be a lot higher than it should be, indicating that it is overvalued. So, what is the P/E ratio that indicates the stock market is fairly valued? Well, historically, the stock market has had an average P/E ratio of 14–15. This means the price of the S&P 500 has been, on average, between 14 and 15 times the average earnings of the index, if we use that index as the benchmark of the stock market as a whole. If this ratio, at some point in time, is under 14, for example, this means the stock market could be moving in the direction of undervaluation and may present good buys, if the trend continues. If the P/E is 16 or above, it could be starting to enter overvalued territory. Just remember, the price/earnings (P/E) ratio indicates the relationship between an equity's (or the stock market's as a whole) earnings and the price the market is willing to pay for those earnings. Another reason the long-term price-earnings ratio average is between 14 and 15 is that 14.5 is the inverse of 6.9% (1 divided by 14.5), which is the long-term inflation-adjusted profit of the stock market. There is an almost perfectly indirect relationship between this long-term P/E ratio and the long-term average inflation-adjusted profit of the stock market (6.9%).

You can find the P/E figures above in the "Market Laboratory" section of *Barron's* weekly financial newspaper. Most public libraries will carry a copy of *Barron's*. Under the column, "Indexes, P/E's, and Yields," you will find the various stock market index P/E ratios. You can also search Google for "current P/E index ratios" to help confirm or quickly find this figure. The internet is probably the easiest and fastest way to get this P/E information. Again, knowing the value of the current P/E ratio is important in order to correctly follow the Buy/Sell Rules of Strategic Stock Accumulation (SSA), which will be explained fully in Chapter 8

Having already discussed the definition and purpose of the P/E ratio (trailing twelve months, or TTM), it is important now to introduce a different valuation version of the stock market using an improved, I believe, variation of the TTM P/E ratio. This is the **P/E-10 ratio that measures the average price-to-earnings ratio over the previous 10 years, adjusted for inflation.** The P/E-10 ratio is taken from the work of the original value investors, Benjamin Graham and David Dodd. They first described this ratio in their classic investment book, "Security Analysis," which was the first book to describe, in detailed, practical terms, so-called "value" investing. This is also called the CAPE ratio (cyclically adjusted price earnings) and the P/E-10 Shiller index. Robert Shiller (Nobel laureate) has repopularized this 10-year version of the P/E ratio since using it extensively in his books and Nobel Prize winning research. The P/E-10 is calculated by taking the annual earnings per share of a stock index such as the S&P 500, for the past 10 years. After adjusting these earnings for inflation by using the consumer price index, the current price level of the S&P 500 is then divided by the ten-year average earnings per share to yield the P/E-10 or CAPE ratio.

The value of the P/E-10 ratio, over and above the trailing 12 months P/E ratio first described, is that the former smooths out the more radical changes in the stock market over time. For example, in 2000, the one-year TTM (trailing twelve months) P/E ratio became excessively high, and therefore useless as a valuation tool, because earnings dropped much faster than stock prices. This resulted in a misleading P/E ratio on the high side. Some P/E ratios at that time were in excess of 100. However, the P/E-10 ratio, indicating the ten-year average, was much more accurate as a forecasting tool since it took into account the previous 10 years, not just one year.

The P/E-10 ratio, rather than the one-year P/E ratio, is the one used to help determine buy and sell decisions in the Strategic Stock Accumulation Strategy. Again, since the long-term stock market P/E ratio is about 14.5, then, if the ten-year average starts to exceed 16 or 17, the market is probably beginning to become overvalued. Yet we can realize that the stock market can remain overvalued for a long time, before a severe market correction or crash occurs. The SSA takes this common occurrence into account, by including rules that keep the investor "long" (owning stock) for a longer period of time, even if the P/E valuation by itself may dictate selling.

The value of the P/E-10 ratio, if 24 or higher, for example, indicates that the stock market is likely to yield low returns overall for a number of years. This is because it will revert to a fairer valuation over time. This reversion will typically result in lower stock prices during this time. This concept is called reversion to the mean (or to the average).

The P/E-10 ratio does not tell an investor when the market will begin its reversion to the mean. In other words, it says nothing about when the stock market will become more fairly valued, only that at some point it will. But, this reversion to the 'average' means it must, out of necessity and at some point, undershoot fair value to ultimately average out (because of its previous overshooting fair value).

So, for our purposes, it only means that we should be ready with our cash and bonds (by converting to cash) to buy stock "on sale," when it happens. It's important to always be invested in stock to some extent. This would be determined by your chosen initial stock/bonds-cash ratio, and the changes in this ratio are determined by the rules of SSA. Always maintain at least the percentage of stock represented by your initially chosen stock/bond-cash ratio. The rules for determining when to buy more stock, and when to sell back to your original stock percentage in your stock/bond-cash ratio, will be explained in the chapter on "STRATEGIC STOCK ACCUMULATION: THE METHOD— Step by Step" in Chapter 8.

As I had said before, the P/E ratio, and specifically the P/E-10 ratio, is the only financial measure necessary to use the rules of SSA. However, I want to describe a number of other stock market valuation tools. These tools are commonly used by stock analysts to help confirm stock or overall stock market valuation. The SSA method uses other methods to determine buying and selling. **If you are interested in learning a little more about how the stock market is valued by some of the so-called "professionals" who do this every day, read on. If not, don't worry about it. Just follow the rules of SSA. As you follow the instructions described in**

Chapter 8, you only need to concern yourself with one financial measure—the P/E-10 ratio, to help determine, along with the other simple rules of SSA, when to buy and sell.

I am including the following terms and concepts, because they will be important to investors as general background stock market information, but they are not necessary to implement SSA successfully.

The knowledge of this information could very well be helpful to many investors mainly as a psychological support during those times when almost everyone else is selling and you need to buy. If you think that you may fall into this category of needing reasonable support, then read this chapter. In other words, the more you know about valuation concepts that will, at some point, affect the stock market, the less likely you will be to "lose heart" and give way to portfolio-destroying "panic selling" (when you should be buying).

Again, if you have a solid grasp of Strategic Stock Accumulation, truly understand and have confidence in its success as a stock market strategy, then the following ratios and concepts are not necessary to be successful. However, being at least familiar with them, in many cases, is a good idea. Just remember, when considering these valuation techniques, they should all be thought of as helpful to determine overall stock market valuation, not to determine valuation of individual stocks. This is because for the purposes of SSA, it is important to get used to thinking in these terms. In the next chapter, I will discuss the importance of always buying index funds that reflect broad market value and never individual stocks. I will, at that time, fully explain the important logical reasons for this.

Price-to-Book Ratio

The Price-to-Book ratio (P/B ratio) is a financial tool used to compare a company's book value to its market price. Book value is a company's (or the stock market's, as a whole) total assets minus its total liabilities; in other words, its net value. This ratio is calculated by dividing the company's current share price by the book value per share. Book value per share is its book value divided by number of outstanding shares. When this ratio starts to exceed 2–3 times by this financial measure, then the stock market is becoming overvalued. This ratio can be effective in helping to determine the value of the stock market, because it shows a direct relationship between asset value and market value. For those who may be interested, this ratio helps to compare P/B ratios within industries, since there is definite valuation variation among them.

Since you will maintain your initial asset allocation by rebalancing, as is called for in the SSA rules, it does not matter to you which industries are overvalued or undervalued, as your primary interest is valuation of the stock market as a whole. As a matter of fact, the rebalancing that will occur regularly within your portfolio (as a result of periodic under and overvaluation of portfolio asset classes) will add further incremental value, over and above the basic SSA Strategy. If this sounds a bit confusing right now, have no worries; this will all be clearly explained in Chapter 6, "Choosing the Index Funds for Your Asset Allocation."

Price-to-Sales Ratio

The price-to-sales ratio (P/S ratio) is used to compare a company's sales to its stock price, measuring its value per dollar of sales. This is probably more reliable than the TTM, non-inflation-adjusted P/E ratio, because a company's sales are less susceptible to cyclical swings than are earnings. The simplest way to calculate this ratio is to divide a company's stock price by the sales per share over a 12 month period. Also known as the sales multiple, it's especially useful in evaluating newer companies with good sales but little or no net income. If the S&P 500 is trading at a lower P/S ratio than its historical average of 1.42, then it indicates undervaluation by this financial measure.

Return on Equity

Return on Equity (ROE) is a very good indicator or of

how well a company is using its assets to create profit. It is calculated by dividing a company's net profit by the average shareholder equity for the period. Shareholder equity is simply assets minus liabilities. How much equity the shareholders have is divided into the company's or industries or stock market net worth to determine return on equity. This number allows investors to cut through the "B.S." in a company's or industry's annual report and get to the heart of the matter. A company, for example, could be highly leveraged. This could result in a misleadingly high ROE, because that would reduce the shareholders' equity in the denominator. A better gauge would be to add the debt to the shareholders' equity in the denominator to show the effectiveness of the capital employed to generate profits. This is called the return of capital employed, or ROCE. This gives the investor a better idea of how management is performing. However, the increased debt levels need to be taken into consideration.

Profit Margin

A gross profit margin is calculated by subtracting cost of goods sold (COGS) from net sales, which yields gross profit. This figure is then divided by the net sales, so that the gross profit margin equals net sales, minus cost of goods sold, divided by net sales. This figure is a good indicator of the pricing power of a company or industry or of the stock market as a whole. For example, is it able to generate greater profits because of lower cost of goods sold or because of diminished competition yielding greater pricing power? Quite often as a strong economy marches on, profit margins begin to decrease as labor costs and price competition both increase. This can be another way to help confirm a stock market getting "long in the tooth."

CapEx

CapEx (capital expenditures) is a term used to describe the capital expenditures a company, industry, or stock market as a whole makes to increase future profits. As an economic expansion progresses, industry will typically spend more money on new equipment, factories, and refurbishing or extending the life of existing assets. So as capex increases, we can see that the economy is more likely to continue, at least for a time, to expand. Of course, this may or may not have a direct relationship with the stock market, since the market not only looks ahead but is subject also to the laws of valuation and reversion to the mean (as discussed earlier).

Sharpe Ratio

The Sharpe ratio is a very popular method of comparing the risk/return probabilities of one return-generating asset with another. Its popularity has a lot to do with its supposed simplicity (yeah, right!) The formula is as follows:

$S(x) = (r_x - R_f) / StdDev(x)$
where
x is some investment
r_x is the average annual rate of return of x (i.e., T-bills)
R_f is the best available rate of return of a "risk-free" security (i.e. cash or Treasury Inflation Protected Securities)
$StdDev(x)$ is the standard deviation of r_x

The equation basically describes alleged excess return an investor receives for the extra risk that he or she accepts for holding a riskier asset. Basically, we subtract the risk-free return of longer-term Treasury inflation-protected securities (TIPS) from the expected average rate of return of any asset with some risk attached to it. We can divide this result by its standard deviation. Standard deviation, in statistics and probability, is the attempt to quantify how much dispersion or variation exists as related to some average. In other words, how much deviation is there from one point to the mean (or "average")?

A high standard deviation means that the data points encompass a large range of values, while a low standard deviation would show these points closer to the mean or expected value. The standard deviation is the square root of its variants. In finance, the standard deviation on the rate of return of an investment is a measure of the volatility of the investment. So for purposes of the Sharpe ratio, the greater the standard deviation or volatility of an asset, as indicated in the denominator of the equation, the lower the Sharpe ratio will be.

If the average rate of return of an asset exceeds that of another asset, but the volatility of the first asset is greater, that fact alone may make investment in the first asset less attractive on a risk-adjusted basis. How can we use this application of the Sharpe ratio for the market as a whole? And, even if we can, does it really matter for our investment purposes? Like all of these other market indicators, it serves a purpose in helping to determine the overall valuation of the stock market. Therefore, it is one more cog in the wheel for the analyst in determining the market's overall value.

Again, for purposes of Strategic Stock Accumulation Strategy, our focus will be on P/E-10 ratios as the only relevant financial measure. So, if you are interested to fill in the values for the Sharpe ratio equation, then you must first predict an expected overall rate of return for the market. Granted, this is an estimate, but it is an estimate based, to some extent, on facts. We would start with the next year's expected gross national product (GNP). To this number, we add the expected dividend rate, then subtract the risk-free rate of return (based on the long-term Treasury inflation-protected securities interest rate [TIPS]), and then divide the result by the overall standard deviation.

You may be thinking right now: "well, if I knew next year's gross domestic product and the dividend rate (and I have a good understanding of stock market valuation tools), then I may already be able to accurately predict next year stock market." Not really! All those numbers would tell you are what the stock market would do if it followed these numbers in a direct linear fashion. It never does! So much depends on how long the market has been overvalued, or undervalued, or subject to so many other possible factors as to make it unpredictable based on one, or even several, yardstick comparisons alone.

So, analysts treat the Sharpe ratio as they do all of the others: Just one more factor to consider. Let's look at an example. If the expected gross domestic product is 4% next year, and the expected overall S&P 500 dividend rate is 2%, then this gives us an overall expected market return of 6%. Then subtract 2.5% (TIPS: long-term interest rate) from the expected 6% market return. This gives us 3.5%. If inflation is 2% percent, then we get an inflation-adjusted extra risk return of 1 1/2% next year.

Can we expect the stock market, given the above figures, to advance 1 1/2% in real terms next year? Hardly! If, for example, in the previous year, the S&P 500 advanced 30% while the expected return was only 4%, then we must factor in the probability of some 'reversion to the mean' occurring this year. This reversion could easily mean that the stock market will now undershoot fair value next year to compensate for overshooting it the previous year.

Also, the longer the stock market remains overvalued or undervalued, all other things being equal (and they never are), the greater the expected volatility or standard deviation in the denominator of the Sharpe ratio. In other words, the longer a bull market lasts, maybe even into a "bubble" territory, the greater the risk of a severe market contraction or crash. So, in your mind, if you are so inclined, simply add next year's economists' average estimate of gross domestic product to the expected dividend rate. Subtract the long-term TIPS (let's say 2.5%), divide this number by a standard deviation that we must admit is highly subjective but could be based on its relation to the previous year's rate. Give it a greater valuation if you perceive the market as overvalued. If the market is undervalued, a higher expected return should help to compensate, to some extent, for the higher volatility (StdDev) in the denominator, and still yield a higher Sharpe ratio.

For the purposes of Strategic Stock Accumulation, all of the above is simply an academic exercise for some investors, possibly a review for others, and probably of little or no interest to most investors. Regardless, understanding this information is not necessary to successfully implement Strategic Stock Accumulation.

Gordon Growth Model

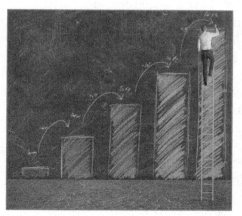

The Gordon Growth Model is a more simplified approach to estimating the next year's total stock market return. I like this one. It's simple and can quickly give a somewhat accurate, but still "ball park" estimate, of how the stock market would do if it was fairly valued in the previous 5 to 10 years, so there would be little or no 'reversion to the mean' to figure in the equation. Then, of course, we have to consider how big a factor "animal spirits" (greed and fear) will have on our prediction. So, assuming no reversion to the mean, no extreme emotional buying or selling, and no extraneous world events affecting the market (e.g., possible "black swan" events—more on this later) then we could make a (not necessarily accurate) prediction of where the stock market would be in one year. Since none of these possibilities can be ruled out, all we can be confident of is using the Gordon Growth Model (GGM) as a starting point. But, that's ok. It's still fun to try and come up with a prediction, based on the GGM and all of these other factors. For purposes of implementing SSA successfully, it doesn't mean anything significant to our final objective.

The GGM says that a stock market's return will be equal to its dividend yield plus its dividend growth rate. Using the S&P 500 as a benchmark to help determine the overall value of the stock market, we would start with, let's say, an overall 2% dividend rate. The tricky part is then in determining the overall dividend growth rate. All we can do is estimate next year's overall S&P 500 dividend growth rate. One way of doing this would be to look at last year's dividend growth rate and then determine if dividend rates have increased or decreased over the last several quarters. If you came to the conclusion dividends would increase by 5% next year, based on the last three-quarters, and the dividend yield now is 2%, the result would be an overall market increase in valuation of 7% by this formula. Of course, we would adjust for inflation to get an inflation-adjusted total return of about 5% if we had a 2% inflation forecast. Again, this is a fast way to make a "back of the envelope" projection for next year's stock market. How accurate it turns out to be is another question, because we have our old friend 'reversion to the mean' to deal with, as well as all of the other unknown factors that will affect the market. As a predictive tool, it is only interesting in helping to provide a somewhat educated guess as to when the next severe correction or crash will occur. When that happens, it does not worry me, (I like it!) nor should it worry you. The only things that matter are having the cash to buy stock index funds, at that point, and following the rules on how to do so, as laid out in Chapter 8..

Q Ratio

The Q ratio is calculated by dividing the market value of a company, or the stock market as a whole, by the replacement cost of the firm's or market's assets:

$$\text{Q Ratio} = \frac{\text{Total Market Value of Company}}{\text{Total Asset Value}}$$

If we were so inclined, we could simply substitute total market figures for individual company numbers to get an estimated total market value. This would give us more information as to where the stock market is in relation to its next correction or crash episode.

Devised by James Tobin of Yale University, Nobel laureate in economics, the Q ratio tested his hypothesis that the total market value of all companies on the stock market should be equal to their replacement costs. Theoretically, therefore, if the Q value is less than 1, this means that the replacement cost of a firm's assets is greater than the value of the stock, implying that the stock is undervalued. Conversely, a value greater than 1 means that the company's stock is probably overvalued. However, the average (arithmetic mean) Q ratio is now 0.68, which would imply the average condition of the stock market is undervaluation, which presently (as of July, 2014) is not true. This is probably because the replacement cost of a firm's assets, unfortunately, on average, is overstated. This is still a well-regarded method by analysts as well as by individual investors for estimating fair market value of a stock or of the overall state of the stock market. The numbers for this calculation are supplied by the *Federal Reserve z.1 Financial Accounts of the United States,* which is released quarterly.

Gold Standard

The "gold standard" is not a financial ratio or measure, just as the terms following it in this chapter are not. I'm including the gold standard as general background information, because it has had such a devastating deflationary effect in the U.S. prior to 1913. This is largely forgotten today, and there are still regular calls among so-called "gold bugs" and other "hard money" advocates to reestablish the gold standard in our country.

The United States had been on some combination of a gold and/or silver standard from 1879-1933, when the federal government stopped the free convertibility of dollars into gold. The total gold stock in the country was nationalized, and the only time gold could be exchanged for dollars after that time was for international transactions. Even this exception was then later abandoned by former President Richard Nixon. All official links of gold to dollars were ended in 1976.

Much of the paper money used under a gold standard is, of course, not gold, but it represents a promise to pay gold. A national bank system was set up in 1863 to ensure that paper money convertibility into gold would be honored. In 1913, the Federal Reserve System was finally set up for several important reasons. One was to make sure check convertibility would be honored, and another was to deal with the periodic severe banking panics and the stock market crashes resulting from massive conversions of accounts into cash.

Between the end of the Civil War and 1913, regular depressions and bank panics seem to be uncontrollable. The Federal Reserve System was set up to lend money to banks on a short-term basis in order to allow banks to continue functioning in the face of large customer requests for their cash. Unfortunately, this new power of the Federal Reserve could not help the U.S. avoid the "Great Depression." Why not? Because of the gold standard.

Massive bank failures occurred again during the period between 1930 and 1933, as the Great Depression set in. The very purpose the Federal Reserve was created in the first place, to provide adequate liquidity to banks, was largely ignored. In order to create the cash necessary to meet the demands of an economy desperate for it, and also to lower interest rates, large amounts of gold would have had to leave the country because of higher returns abroad. The Fed had a choice: expand the money supply and lose gold, or stay on the gold standard and further contract the economy (and exacerbate the depression). It chose, at first, to stay on the gold standard. The Depression got worse.

Finally, as the worldwide depression continued, Great Britain and several other countries came off of the gold standard. The U.S., under President Franklin Roosevelt, followed suit in 1933. Now the Fed could provide liquidity without having to worry about gold reserves, which were simply nationalized. It became against the law for private individuals to own gold. Economic contractions since then have been much less severe, notwithstanding the severe stock market drops of 2000 and 2008–2009. There is no question that had we been on a gold standard in 2007, a depression would have ensued, as the same negative economic forces of the 1930's would have been set into motion again.

And yet, we still hear today about how foolish we were to go off of the gold standard, and about how the gold standard forces discipline on the politicians and the market. Well, I would advise anyone not sure about this to do some research on the history of the gold standard up to the 1930s and much of the 1800s. There were regular, numerous banking collapses and even more severe stock market crashes occurring after the Civil War up to the early 20th century. We still have economic recessions and stock market crashes; yes, some are severe. But, at least the banks don't lose our money (up to insured limits), and as bad as 2008-9 was, we didn't see any bread lines or people jumping from tall buildings.

John Maynard Keynes called gold "the barbarous relic," and so it is. I am sharing these history points about gold with you simply because you will hear calls for its reestablishment in the financial press and in the secular media from time to time. If you didn't already have some idea concerning the history of the "gold standard," you do now. All I can say to those looking longingly at the good old days of gold-standard-forced monetary discipline on our government, read some 19th century U.S. economic history, and be careful what you wish for.

Percentages

 Another concept to understand and become familiar with is the mathematical term of "percentages." Many people have trouble thinking easily in terms of percentages. If you did not pick this up somewhere in school, it would be helpful to do so now. In working with percentages, all you need to be able to do is multiply and divide. If you don't have the multiplication tables memorized up to 12×12, you can always use a calculator.

For example, you may be trying to figure out if the market as a whole is projected to go up 15% in the next year, how much your stock index fund ETF investments within your SSA portfolio will increase, if this projection proves true. To do this, you simply multiply your total stock investments by 1.15. And to the extent that your stock index ETF mirrors the overall market, that is what your stock return will be. For many people, this is an elementary school lesson. For others not used to this, it's good to practice thinking through percentage terms in your head. Maybe even look up the multiplication tables on the internet to 12 times 12 and start memorizing them.

Anyone with the intelligence to understand the SSA method, which isn't difficult, I promise, can learn to work with percentages. Get used to playing around with percentages on a calculator, if not in your head.

The other common example where percentages are important is as follows: let's say your stock (not bonds or cash) investments have gone up $9000 last year, and you had $87,000 total stock in your account at the beginning of last year. Now, you want to find out what you're percent gain on your total stock investments was last year. Well, you would simply divide $9000 by $87000, to get 10.3%. In other words, you got a 10.3% return on your stock market investments last year.

One more example: let's say the S&P 500 is at 1500, and many stock analysts think that the market will increase by 12% next year. Again, we would multiply 1500 × 1.12, to get 1680, which is what the S&P 500 would end up at for the year, if those analysts' projections were right. So, again, in your case, you would simply multiply your own stock value, whatever it is, by 1.12, to get an idea of how your own stock investments would be affected if this projection proves true. When you understand percentages, you can easily make these simple projections for your portfolio.

I think many people are intimidated into thinking that there is no way they can handle their own stock market investments. One of these reasons, I think, is the lack of experience of thinking in terms of simple percentages. Once you get used to thinking this way, it becomes easier to estimate and "round number" your future stock market results (based on any projection) in your head. It becomes fun, once you get used to it. As I said, if you aren't interested in this mental exercise, there is no problem as far as SSA is concerned; simply use a calculator.

The Federal Reserve

The Federal Reserve is the 'gatekeeper' of the U.S. economy. The "Fed," as it is commonly referred to, has such a direct relationship to the short-term direction of the stock market that knowledge of how it operates would be helpful for your overall understanding of the stock market. The Federal Reserve regulates the nation's financial institutions and is responsible for the smooth functioning of the U.S. economy.

That has proven to be a difficult task, at the present, in our capitalistic free-market economy, largely because it must now also compensate for the fiscal inactivity of the U.S. Congress. When Congress fails to perform this function responsibly, the Fed comes under increasing pressure. The Congress has had no credible budget passed for years. The budget deficit that results is atrocious. Regardless, the Fed tries to fulfill its mandate as closely as possible.

There are 12 Federal Reserve Banks and a number of branches. Since it is an independent body, it does not need the approval of any other branches of the federal government to carry out the actions that it decides upon. However, the chairman must periodically testify before Congress concerning its outlook and actions. The Fed is supposed to be free from political pressure. This hasn't always been the case. All board members are nominated by the President and approved by the Senate. According to the Federal Reserve's website, its purpose is to "promote sustainable growth, high levels of employment, stability of prices to help preserve the purchasing power of the dollar, and moderate long-term interest rates." The Fed is also involved in clearing checks and distributing coin and paper money to the nation's banks, credit unions, and savings and loan associations. The Fed also frequently handles the electronic transfer of money.

The Federal Reserve conducts research on the national and regional economic situation. The results of this research are released to the public through speeches, published articles, and websites. This is all part of the responsibility of the Federal Reserve.

The Federal Reserve was created by law in 1913 with passage of the Federal Reserve Act and signing by President Woodrow Wilson. A previous central bank ended in 1836 when then-President Andrew Jackson refused to renew its charter, because he believed it had too much power and was controlled by the "rich Eastern Establishment." The country lived with the severe negative banking effects of that decision for over 75 years.

President Jackson was considered by some to be a "man of the people," and he distrusted the centralized power of the national bank at that time. The effects of a lack of any central banking control led to a series of banking collapses, which in turn, led to stock market crashes in 1873, 1893, and a very serious one in 1907. These bank failures resulted in many people losing their life savings. Congress was finally forced to push again for a centralized banking system.

In 1913, a new law was passed, which has given the Fed its mandate to the present day. Let's look a little closer at this mandate. The Fed engages in what are called "open market operation." We'll look at this in more detail a little later, but these 'operations' allow the Fed to affect interest rates. The Fed has historically affected interest rates largely by controlling the discount rate (it also has other options to accomplish this goal). This is the interest rate that banks must pay to borrow money from the Federal Reserve.

Why would banks want to borrow money from the Fed? Because banks need to keep a certain amount of money in reserve, just in case a lot of people want their deposited money back all at one time. This is one advantage of having a powerful central bank. It can be thought of as a giant banking insurance company. If the above were to actually happen, the Fed can always step in and lend unlimited amounts of money to banks under such circumstances.

The absence of a central bank before 1913 meant that when there were more bank customers wanting their money back than there was money available (because most of it was lent out to borrowers), everybody lost because the bank then went bankrupt, and all depositors were paid only a fraction, if that, of their deposited money. For this reason, banks now require a certain level of reserves at all times. This amount of reserves is determined by the Federal Reserve and changes periodically, based on the condition of the economy.

The Fed always stands ready to lend banks money, when necessary. The Fed can raise or lower the reserve requirements of individual banks. If the reserve requirements are lowered, this means that banks can keep less money on their books and lend more of what they have to businesses, individuals, and other banks. This decrease in reserve requirements has the effect of increasing the money supply, because more money is then lent out and in circulation in the economy. The Fed can also affect the economy and interest rates by what is called "quantitative easing." This involves the Fed injecting larger amounts of money into the economy by purchasing large amount of bonds regularly in the various bond markets, which I'll discuss in more detail later in this chapter.

Federal Open Market Committee (FOMC)

The Federal Open Market Committee is part of the Federal Reserve and meets eight times a year. This Committee determines and sets interest rates while also deciding on any changes needed in the overall money supply by using the different operations as discussed above.

The FOMC has 12 members, which includes 7 members of the Board of Governors, the President of the Federal Reserve Bank of New York, and 4 of the other 11 Reserve Bank Presidents. The four reserve bank presidents serve one-year terms on a rotating basis.

Now, let's look at these "open market operations" in the context of our free-market capitalistic economic system. You will hear from time to time, in the financial press or on TV business programs (such as CNBC's morning financial program—"Squawk Box"), that the Fed wishes to "stimulate the economy." This is undertaken in response to what it sees as a slowing economy, resulting in unacceptable job losses. What the Fed wants to do in this situation is to lower overall interest rates in order to make it easier for corporations and individuals to borrow money for business, cars, homes, etc., and to also make it easier to pay these loans back. This also has the net result of increasing corporate profits directly. This occurs because the interest expense of the corporations' outstanding loans are reduced, thereby improving the bottom line (i.e., net profits).

This improving profit picture for corporations will, hopefully, lead to a rising stock market. It is sometimes said that corporate profits are the "mother's milk of a rising stock market." When the stock market rises, stock investors feel richer, and they spend more money on homes, cars, businesses, etc. This does seem like a virtuous cycle to many investors. It's also true that an increase in interest rates will eventually have the opposite effect... more about that later.

So, how does the Fed accomplish this goal of stimulating the economy by using this tool of open market operations? As I said, this is usually the first thing that they try. These lower interest rates then occur as a result of these open market operations but have been slow to have their desired effect on the overall economy (during this latest so-called "Great Recession," starting in 2008) until just recently. As of July, 2014, new jobs are finally starting to increase to over 200,000 per month, while the unemployment rate has decreased to 6.2%.

So, this is how open market operations are conducted:

banks lend out most of their money or usually do. They are required, however, by the Fed, to keep a certain amount of their money in reserve, as explained earlier, just in case large numbers of people come in and want their deposited money back. Their customer deposits are what the banks lend out at higher interest rates than what they have paid to their depositors. If one bank is getting short on reserves, it will borrow an amount of money from another bank overnight so that it is in compliance with its reserve requirements. The interest rate that the bank pays the lending bank is what is called the "overnight interest rate," and it can change from day to day. Let's say that the overnight rate is 3% on an annual basis. This would, of course, only be a fraction of 3% on an overnight basis.

Now, if the Fed wants to lower interest rates to stimulate the economy, it will, at first, engage in the following type of open market operations: it will print money and use this money to buy short-term treasury bonds. By short term, I mean one year or less, before the bond becomes due for payment. The interest rate on these bonds is less than longer-term bonds, because there is less inflation risk in a short-term bond. In other words, if the bond investor wants to buy a 30 year bond, for example, he will almost always require a higher interest rate to compensate for the risk that inflation will cause his bond investment to be worth a lot less in 30 years. A short-term bond has much less time or duration risk from inflation associated with it.

So, the Fed buys these short-term bonds with money it has printed, and this money goes into the hands of those who previously owned the short-term bonds. These investors then deposit the money that they received from the sale of their bonds into various banks, thereby increasing the cash available to those banks to make additional loans. This also increases the money supply. Now that these banks have more money, they don't need to borrow as much from other banks or the Federal Reserve to fulfill their reserve requirements. This results in a decrease in the demand for overnight loans, while increasing the supply of dollars available for overnight loans.

The decreased demand for overnight loans and

increased supply of available dollars for overnight loans leads to a decrease in short-term interest rates (law of supply and demand), which is the Fed's goal. What the Fed would like to happen is for interest rates higher up on the curve (longer-term interest rates) to also decrease. Ideally, this will happen as a result of the lower short-term rates. This doesn't always go according to plan, as was the case after 2008 when the Fed was forced to try another approach called quantitative easing (or QE), which I'll explain nex

Quantitative Easing

Quantitative easing, or QE, as it is known, can be thought of as an open market operations strategy "on steroids." Instead of simply buying short-term bonds and thereby injecting money into the economy by this means, the Fed can use a "bazooka" approach by informing investors beforehand that it will print a predetermined large amount of money and inject it into the economy, directly to the banks, usually on a regular monthly basis. The Fed does this by buying not only short-term bonds with these newly printed dollar but also longer-term bonds; specifically, it buys what are called mortgage backed securities and commercial debt. This also has the effect of pretty much forcing longer-term interest rates down.

Our previous chairman, Ben Bernanke, called this process "credit easing," instead of the more popular term, "quantitative easing." During most of 2013, $85 billion per month was injected into the U.S. economy in this manner. That came to about $1 trillion per year in an economy that already had outstanding debt of $16 trillion. He, and the rest of the voting Fed governors, were trying to target certain areas of the economy, like home loans (mortgage backed securities), and commercial lending (commercial debt) that were slower to respond to the stimulus caused by the traditional open market operations.

I can hear many readers asking: "How will all of this information about the Fed help me in the stock market?" Well, one fact I cited could be focused on by anyone interested in how all of this debt could affect the stock market. I said that $1 trillion a year is being injected into the U.S. economy. This money has to go somewhere, and much of it will end up in the stock market, causing it to go up in value (at least for a while).

"Okay," you say, "but won't I make most of my money buying stock 'on sale' when the market goes down"? Yes, you will. But, you also make money as it goes up over the long term, and the more it overshoots its true value, then the further down it is likely to go in a market crash or correction (i.e., reversion to the mean). That's when the stage is set to buy undervalued stock on sale, resulting in substantial profits as the market retraces back toward its previous high (and then above that point). You also benefit from the dividends and internal rebalancing while you wait.

Also, Bernanke (and now Yellen) and the Fed have been engaged in the strategy of so-called "financial repression" to slow down bank lending for some time now. This is in contrast to what the present administration claims. Banks are blamed for not lending out enough of their money. The fact is that the large increase in bank regulation since the start of the "Great Recession" has limited the ability of banks to make loans, even to qualified customers. This situation serves the inflation-limiting goals of the Fed and the U.S. government. If the banks start lending full boar again, this could very well heat up the economy too fast. With a $17 trillion U.S. debt to be concerned about, fighting a severe inflation by the Fed's increasing of interest rates (through open market operations) would only exacerbate the debt problem. Of course, the very low interest rates that accompany this financial repression are very good for the stock market. On the other hand, it is very bad for savers (money market funds, certificates of deposits [CDs], and passbook savings accounts).

This financial repression will take the form of vastly increased bank regulation over a considerable period of time and low interest rates. Banks will be forced, in one way or the other, to limit significantly the amount of lending that they can engage in. This serves the purpose of an inflation-concerned Fed. The government will never admit this, but that is what is happening. As a matter of fact, the government criticizes the banks for not lending out their money more freely. This is only for public consumption—politics!

The government cannot allow the economy to expand too fast as a result of greatly expanded bank lending, even if that lending is based on strong loan underwriting. This, the Fed hopes, will have the effect of maintaining the economy on a slower road of growth indefinitely, which would allow it (i.e., the U.S. government) to pay down its debt easier at lower-market interest rates. Again, the government doesn't admit this, choosing instead to emphasize its desire to simply keep interest rates low for consumers and business and also to keep uncontrolled bank lending and speculating in check. That also is true.

This greatly increased bank regulation (Dodd-Frank) would have, in theory, a very moderating future effect on inflation, regardless of national debt levels. At any rate, enjoy the large gains in the stock market and the effect it has on your stock position. And also, at some point in the future, be ready to take advantage of the resulting correction or crash. Former Fed Chairman Bernanke and the present Fed Chairman Janet Yellen want to make all stockholders feel richer by "juicing" the stock market with all of this injected money.

Some believe that at some point the "chickens will come home to roost," and the true value of stocks based on their earnings will be manifested. The near-term future trajectory that the stock market will take is debatable. Others believe that the Federal Reserve can simply use open market operations to moderate the stock market correction or crash that will inevitably occur. I'm skeptical. It will be during this time that you should be able to take advantage of any crash or severe correction by strategically buying large amounts of stock "on sale."

There are some stock and bond managers today, like Bill Gross, former CEO of the giant bond trading firm, Pimco, that believe the economy will be in a "new neutral" situation (Gross had coined the term) for a "long" period of time. Gross' former employer, Pimco, has been the most successful bond investment firm of recent years, at least in terms of client base. This "new neutral" situation would be caused in large part by the maintenance of a "0" real Federal Funds interest rate for years to come. This Federal Funds interest rate is the shortest (and the first) interest rate the Fed targets. Even though the Federal Reserve would maintain a 2% nominal interest rate after inflation is taken into account, the "real" interest rate (if inflation is 2%) would then be "0".

This new neutral environment would be good for both stocks and bonds, but the future returns of both would be limited, in this view. Gross and others believe that the risk of a market crash would be lower. I am skeptical that "this time it's different," and a market crash can be avoided by this so-called "new neutral." Even if a market crash is avoided, it is simply not possible for stock market valuation to stay elevated indefinitely without a correction to fair value. And a correction to fair value would have to involve a drop in the market to undervaluation initially. In other words, overvaluation added to undervaluation eventually equals fair value. Be prepared, at any rate, with your substantial bonds-cash position to buy stock when it is on sale during the next crash or correction.

Another term you that may have heard about in the financial media is "tightening" or "Fed tightening." This simply means the process whereby the Fed slows down its efforts in quantitative easing, finally ends it, and then starts to increase interest rates. The Fed has been reducing the quantitative easing process by $10 billion per month for about 6 months now (as of July, 2014), and this whole QE process should be concluded by October or November 2014. At some point after that, sometime within the next year, the Fed will begin raising the federal funds rate, by its own admission. There is considerable debate concerning where the Fed will end this process of federal funds interest rate increases once it starts. The stock and bond markets appear to be factoring in a nominal federal funds interest rate of about 4%. To get a true interest rate, again, we must subtract the inflation rate. This would result in a true federal funds rate of 2%, for example.

New neutral advocates, however, as stated earlier, believe that the true rate will be 0%, because they believe the Fed will stop raising this rate at about 2% nominal. We can see how this would be good for the stock market. Lower interest rates mean less competition for the stock market from the bond market and higher corporate profits.

Another question open for debate is whether the Federal Reserve will be forced to start unwinding all of this extra money in the economy as the economy starts to pick up speed. Some believe that this will not be necessary, as the continued government policy of severe and relentless bank regulation will have a countervailing effect on inflation. So maybe the Fed will not need to go as high as 4% nominal, at least not for the near term (and maybe not for a long time). This, however, does not mean a stock market crash or severe correction can, or will, be avoided.

We have only to look at what the Federal Reserve did after World War II to see that this financial repression is indeed possible to maintain for long periods of time. Extremely high levels of debt resulted from that war effort, but the Fed was still able to keep interest rates low for quite a while (at least 10 years) after that, as this debt was being unwound, without igniting inflation.

The traditional way that all of this injected money is removed from the economy is by selling the previously bought bonds. The money that it receives for the bonds is removed from the economy, leading to the effect of "tightening" liquidity and slowing economic activity. This is the tight rope that the Fed will be forced to walk. If it tightens too quickly, it could stop economic expansion in its tracks, and another recession could result. This is politically, as well as economically, very unappealing. If the Fed waits too long, inflation could get out of control, which is also an extremely unpopular result all around.

What typically would cause the Fed to unwind its huge bond purchases? Why should they attempt this at all, under any conditions? Why not just leave the extra dollars in the economy? After all, quantitative easing did ultimately bring us out of the recession. It lifted house and stock prices, and finally reduced unemployment, didn't it? Or is it possible that all of these economic improvements would have occurred eventually anyway, just through normal free-market activity? Possibly, but not likely, in my opinion.

I am much more confident in the stock market investment strategy, SSA, than I am about the accuracy of any opinion on this question or any other involving these kinds of economic questions. This is an important point. These questions need only be academic exercises for all of us. Interesting questions, yes (maybe only for some), but that's all! Part of the elegance of Strategic Stock Accumulation Strategy means that it stands on its own, regardless of what the economy or the stock market does. Why this is so will be fully explained in the coming chapters.

Here's another purely academic (for our purposes) question: what if inflation starts to increase to unacceptable levels, in spite of the best efforts of the Federal Reserve to slow down banking activity? Right now, in July of 2014, inflation is running at about 2%. As the economy continues to gain speed resulting from all of that money sloshing through the economy, it is possible inflation could start getting out of hand before the Fed can get a handle on it. In that case, the Fed would definitely be in a quandary. How would it bring down inflation, as I had said, without increasing interest rates and possibly pushing the economy back into recession? One possibility is that the Federal Reserve will begin to tolerate a higher rate of inflation.

The stock market is a forward-looking mechanism, and it will see this potential problem clearly, should inflation start rising. If it even starts to get a whiff of Fed laxity on inflation, interest rates could rise quickly, as the so-called "bond vigilantes" go into action. These bond investors will not tolerate inflation eating away at the value of those assets. They will sell longer-term bonds quickly, raising interest rates on their own. They are called bond vigilantes because of the effectiveness of their demands for higher interest rates on bonds (by refusing to buy lower interest bonds); a demand that the Federal Reserve cannot thwart effectively.

At any rate, at the first sign of Federal Reserve tightening or action by the bond vigilantes, the stock market will probably react, and not the way most investors (but good for SSA investors) would like. In the short run, inflation is not good for the stock market. It cheapens corporate profits by making the dollar worth less. Not to mention the threat of higher interest rates affecting the corporate interest expense negatively, and therefore, corporate profits. However, over the long-term, stocks are a good inflation hedge as corporations are able to pass on rising prices to their customers.

So, enjoy the stock market's exuberance right now, for the dividends and overall increase it causes in the value of your portfolio. At the same time, be prepared for the inevitable future stock market correction or crash by maintaining your significant bond-cash level. I will explain a lot more on that later, step by step, when covering the details of Strategic Stock Accumulation in Chapter 8.

The Debt Ceiling

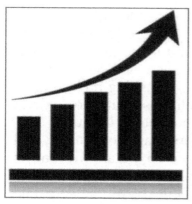

The debt ceiling is a term that is regularly discussed in the financial and secular media. This so-called debt ceiling tends to cause perennial fighting between the Republicans and Democrats in the Congress. This ceiling limits the amount of money the government can borrow. Congress sets the limit, which is now over $17 trillion. Unfortunately, taxes usually are not enough to pay all the outstanding bills incurred by the government. Almost every year, Congress authorizes more spending legislation than taxes can cover. Congress can vote for this debt ceiling to be raised. If that happens, then the government has to borrow as it goes past the previous debt limit. If the limit is not raised, this would cause big problems, because the money has already been allocated to pay bills. Paying all of these bills without the debt ceiling being raised is impossible. The government can't borrow and incur more debt without legislation. So, spending must be cut at that point to be covered by tax receipts. This decrease in government spending can lead to a recession, loss of jobs, and additional undesirable consequences.

If government spending is not reduced and the limit is not raised, then the lack of sufficient money to pay the debt can lead to default, which would cause the U.S. government credit rating to be reduced. This, in turn, would lead to higher interest rates, probably worldwide. Since the U.S. dollar is considered the reserve currency of the world, a loss of confidence in it would have disastrous international repercussions. In fact, the U.S. government would not be able to pay about a third of its bills. This represents about 6.5% of U.S. gross national product and would definitely cause a severe contraction in economic activity. This would lead to a severe correction or crash in the stock market, if not corrected very soon thereafter. Guess what we (SSA investors) would be doing at that point?

How could this situation be corrected? Well, it can probably never be completely corrected. The damage regarding the U.S. credit rating would probably already be done, at least partially. But, economic Armageddon would probably be avoided if the debt ceiling were to be raised soon after the default. The U.S. just doesn't want to go there. So, it often will always be raised, just in time, at the 11th hour. Why would the debt ceiling being raised, when necessary, ever be in question? Why would the U.S. Congress ever risk such a situation as to not pass an increase in the debt ceiling, so that all of its bills can be paid on time?

The answer to the above question involves a basic philosophical difference between liberals and conservatives. Liberals are not averse to spending increases, because they believe most are for important causes, and should be covered, when necessary, by increased taxes. Nor are they concerned about moderate inflation, especially if it is a choice between that and maintaining what they believe is appropriate government spending levels. Conservatives believe that less spending and less taxes are better for the economy and ultimately for all citizens. Many of them believe that this is true even during those times the economy needs more stimulus, as happens during a severe recession.

The House of Representatives has the "power of the purse," and can deny an increase in the debt limit if they wish, even after the money has already been allocated to be spent by the entire Congress. At this time, the "House" is controlled by Republicans, and they periodically threaten to refuse to approve money for what they believe is out-of-control spending. Philosophically, they may be correct, but not when this includes the threat to cause a default in U.S. government bonds by refusing to raise the debt limit. The Republicans have done this to gain leverage in future negotiations to cut the budget deficit and slow down the increase in the national debt, which is now $16 trillion. They always eventually give in though, and ultimately approve the increased debt ceiling.

Regardless of which side you come down on, it helps to be aware of this political conflict that is becoming more and more frequent. Almost everyone is aware these days that some members of Congress are not even civil with some other members; there is a real dislike on the part of the more extreme members of each party for members on the other side. Some believe that unless this is corrected, our country's future economic and political security is at stake. Maybe, but maybe not! But this is why a basic knowledge of U.S. history is so important.

The Founding Fathers, who are so often cited as agreeing or disagreeing themselves (i.e., claiming as constitutional or unconstitutional) over proposed law or even settled law, fought like cats and dogs. The country survived quite well. Some of the members of Congress of the first 30 to 40 years of our Republic truly hated some members of the opposed political party. A dual to the death was actually fought between a former Vice-President of our country,

Aaron Burr, and the Secretary of the Treasury, Alexander Hamilton. Hamilton was killed by Burr in that dual. It can be argued that the conflict between Burr and Hamilton is proof of what can happen when the opposing political parties cannot come to agreement on the most important of issues. Yes, it is rare yet true that some few tragic situations did sometimes happen.

Since dueling was outlawed in the later 1800s, that type of extreme conflict resolution is unlikely to be repeated. Let's consider: Is extreme political conflict within a democracy acceptable? This can be an important and sometimes necessary part of democracy. The bottom line is that in spite of political rancor, it so much better than internal military conflict. Revolution and civil war has, so often in the past, been used by non-democracies to settle these disagreements. Of course, even that type of conflict has not been completely avoided in our nation's history, with the Civil War being the exception.

Democracy (actually, meaning a republic with representative government) has kept the peace within our country, with that one exception, for all the years pre- and post-Civil War. Democracy has also kept the peace within Europe, for the first time in its history. This has only happened because, since World War II, a democratic union of all European Nations was thought correctly to be the only way to avoid war between those nations every 20 years or so.

Had the "extreme" members of Congress not insisted upon stopping the spread of slavery into the new U.S. territories, how much longer would slavery have existed, even in those states where it was already legal and entrenched? In that case, internal military conflict (even within a democracy) proved to be unavoidable.

There I go again—another history lesson. Sorry, I can't help myself. The bottom line is, I don't worry, and you shouldn't either about how political conflict affects the stock market in this country. Conflict, and arguments over the debt ceiling, will be resolved and the U.S. will continue to lead the world in all the important areas.

That's why, even though many non-Americans criticize our country, many of these same people, if given the chance, would still come here in a heartbeat for medical care, college education, or simply a better life for themselves and their children. What do those facts tell us?

CHAPTER 4: Exchange-Traded (Index) Funds

First of all, I would advise never to invest in individual stocks. It doesn't matter how good the story is or what a bargain everyone says is going to occur with companies such as Apple or Facebook. There are too many things that can go wrong, of which you will have neither knowledge of nor control over: everything from fraud charges being brought against top executives, to expropriation of company assets by a foreign country, to such poor performance that the company ends in bankruptcy with little or no warning to stockholders.

I'm not saying that money cannot be made buying individual stocks. Since the stock market, as a whole, increases in value over time, that is certainly possible. It is not a zero-sum game in which there has to be a loser for every winner, although it is frequently described as such. It is true that in every stock transaction, either the buyer or seller will come out ahead in the short term. Over time, theoretically, there should be more winners than losers, unlike a zero-sum game. The long-term individual stock investor, assuming he doesn't overtrade or pay too much in transaction or management costs, can come out ahead over time. The fact that this is possible does not make it probable!

Simply investing in the stock market is a necessary, but not sufficient, cause of long-term wealth. On the other hand, the Strategic Stock Accumulation Strategy can be such a sufficient cause, as you will be able to see clearly in Chapters 8 and 9.

Individual stocks are much more predictably profitable when included within a grouping of stocks, not individually by themselves. There are several significant problems connected with investing in individual stocks, as opposed to index mutual funds with low fees (I'll talk about index funds in more detail shortly). First, there are the problems with the unknown, over and above not knowing how profitable the company will be, such as: fraud, other "problems" with "key" employees, confiscation of assets by an unfriendly foreign country, and non-disclosure of negative financial information concerning the company are some that immediately come to mind. Any of these "surprises" can, and often do, blindside investors.

One way to help alleviate the risk inherent in individual stocks is to buy enough companies' stock in different sectors of the economy to diversify away individual stock risks as much as possible. But isn't this what a managed mutual fund does anyway? So are you are saying that I can do better than a managed mutual fund? Yes, you can! After all, you won't have disgruntled investors demanding you sell their stock when you think that selling will be a mistake. You won't have upwards of 50 or more stocks to watch closely as is the responsibility of a professional fund manager. And finally, you would hopefully be a long-term investor, not one with a short-term bias, as many mutual fund managers have. They are under pressure to deliver results 'yesterday' for their clients. Wait a minute! Haven't I just helped to make the case for individual stocks over all mutual-type funds? Not at all, as I'll continue to explain.

Aside from the potential problems mentioned at the beginning of this chapter that frequently blindside individual stock investors (and those are BIG PROBLEMS), there is another one everyone should be aware of: Time Required. To become a successful long-term investor in individual stocks requires a lot of time. I don't care what anyone says about just being diversified or doing your research. To effectively, consistently pick profitable stocks takes both a lot of time and plenty of effective research. Here's the problem with simply being diversified and doing your own research: You are competing with hundreds of thousands of others who are doing the same thing. Many of these other investors are the so-called professional money managers, with Ivy League MBAs. Many have experience working at the top stock and bond trading houses, such as Goldman-Sachs and Morgan-Stanley. And they are workaholics! Will your research measure up to theirs?

Even if your research shows that Apple, Facebook, and Amazon are all great companies, most of this information is already 'in the market.' And guess who put it in the market: all of those MBAs just mentioned. In other words, they saw the value before you did when those stocks were indeed undervalued. Now, even though they are still great companies, those stocks are fairly valued, and you lost the profit opportunity. The stock market is not rigged illegally against the "little guy," but the unfortunate fact is that it is rigged legally, you might say, because of the differences in investment competence.

"But I'm making out like a bandit right now," you say. "My portfolio is up 30% this year." There's an old very true adage on Wall Street: "Never confuse genius with a bull market." There are many geniuses in the stock market right now. And they will continue to be geniuses until they're not. Then they will simply be sorry. What the market gives, it can take away, usually even faster, once a correction starts. Wow! It sounds now like I'm really down on the stock market, doesn't it? Not at all. Because with my method you will make just as much, if not more, as a result of stock market crashes as during bull markets. Read on!

So, how do you avoid these individual company catastrophes as an investor? There is a very simple way. Just make sure that if one company you own is a victim of one of the above negative scenarios, that there are many others you own in the same group to neutralize the blow. I emphasize <u>many</u> others. You can accomplish this by simply buying a stock fund that invests in many different companies. This is known generally as a mutual fund-type company. However, stay away from mutual funds that have active managers deciding which stocks to buy and sell within the fund. Buy an "index" fund instead!

At least 75-90% of mutual fund "professional managers" cannot even match the overall stock market average in any given year. Over a 10-year period, their record is much worse, with probably less than 3% beating the S&P 500 index. This is an atrocious record, especially if you are paying good money in the form of high expense ratios and expect market-beating performance. You will not get it, unless your investment manager is very lucky.

"I thought that you were raving about how smart and educated most of these professional managers are just a few paragraphs earlier," you say? Yes, they are smart and well-educated. But just because they are smart enough to beat most individual investors, doesn't make them smart enough to match the average stock market returns. How can this be? There are two reasons: one is "transaction costs"—commission costs to buy and sell stock within the fund. The other reason is high 'expense ratios.' They are the fees the brokerage firms charge investors to manage the fund.

After these two fees are taken out of any profits, it is very difficult for an investment manager to beat the market with your money. Both of these costs delete significant value from the fund over time. There is another reason it is almost impossible for any of them to even match the stock market returns over a ten-year period or longer, and that is that they are competing against all of the other smart and well-educated professional managers who manage all of the other mutual funds. Basically, they are competing against themselves, so it is impossible as a group for them all to beat themselves. **You can do better than the vast majority of them on your own with SSA. I will show you how!**

Forget about looking for some "professional manager" to consistently pick the right stocks in your fund. A fool's errand is certainly found in trying to find the managers who exceed the stock market average in any one year, and especially over longer time periods of time. Most of the time, market-beating results have more to do with luck than skill. Over 10 years or more, almost all of these "hot hands" will revert back to below market average performance. Meanwhile, you have paid hundreds of dollars extra in expense ratio and transaction cost fees. With an actively managed fund, you not only pay a certain percentage of your funds value every year for usually subpar management performance (this, on average, costs more than 1% of the money that you have invested in a typical managed fund per year!), but every time the manager buys and sells stock within the fund, you pay commission for the transaction! The average managed fund has a stock turnover of up to 100% or more. This means you pay the commission for almost every stock in the fund, on average, to be bought and sold every year! Totally ridiculous and unnecessary!

On some level, these fund companies emphasizing active management of funds have to believe that "there's a sucker born every minute." How do we avoid these management and transaction fees and still capture close to, or more than, 100% of the stock market return (which is much easier to accomplish without all of those fees)?We do this by buying only a group of stocks (or bonds), which have been pre-chosen to replicate, as closely as possible, a given industry or particular stock market benchmark (such as the S&P 500)—an index fund with almost no turnover. Most of these funds also have super-low costs (if you pick the right ones—a simple task) for expense ratios, because they need almost no management. That is because the stocks within the fund rarely change, and so there is very little stock turnover (i.e., sales of stock) within the fund. This keeps costs down as low as .05% (that's 5/100 of 1%!), as in the case of Vanguard's S&P 500 index fund. Many actively managed funds will charge expense ratios of more than 1% per year, not including transaction costs, most of the time, for subpar performance.

If you listen to the financial news programs regularly, you will occasionally hear the comment "this is a stock picker's market." What they are saying, and trying to convince you of, is that since the stock market as a whole is not moving up but is in a trendless mode; you must be good enough to pick individual stocks that may buck the trend of the market in order to make money during this time. This is pure B.S. Most of them are not good enough to accomplish this feat. This is always said to justify an entire industry built up around giving investment advice. After all, if everyone simply bought low-cost index funds instead of individual stocks or managed funds, then why would any of these people (i.e., investment managers who want to sell their services) ever be necessary?

Let me make one thing clear. I will never give purchase advice about individual stocks or even individual index funds, except to say, "buy low-cost index funds of your choosing for your stock and bond asset allocation." I have included 8 to 10 types of stock index funds (for either Asset Allocation A- Chart 1 or B- Chart 2) in Chapter 6, "Choosing the Index Funds for Your Asset Allocation." All of this will be explained in that chapter. You must choose which specific market or brokerage index funds to buy for your portfolio. The same goes for the bond index funds in the bond-cash portion of your portfolio.

Having said this, I do believe that Vanguard is the best discount brokerage for any investor's money, although I'm certainly no better than anyone else in advising which stocks (within a fund) to buy. Many individual investors are always looking for a stock market "guru" to advise them. They are constantly searching for the newest "hot hand." It amazes me that many investors will put their life savings in the hands of someone they barely know, simply because he calls himself a "professional manager" and has had about three years or so of outstanding results.

Let's think about the stock-picking ability of some of these hotshot fund managers in terms of statistics. If you flip a coin 10 times, what are the odds that it will come up heads 10 times in a row? Well, the odds are $1/2$ times $1/2$ = $1/4$ times $1/2$ = $1/8$ times $1/2$ = $1/16$ times $1/2$ = $1/32$ times $1/2$ = $1/64$ times $1/2$ = $1/128$ times $1/2$ = $1/256$ times $1/2$ = $1/512$ times $1/2$ = $1/1,024$ times $1/2$ = 2,048 So, the odds of flipping heads 10 times in a row are 1 out of 2,048. Not very good odds, are they? **But, there are now more mutual funds out there (and therefore, thousands of fund**

managers) than there are individual stocks listed on all the exchanges.

So, we can then see how it is not only possible, but probable, that every few years there will be a certain small number of these fund managers that come up with heads at least 5 to 7 times in a row. **Statistically, it must happen, just by luck alone.** It is very important for your financial survival to understand the previous statement. It will be by luck alone! They will have stellar results for maybe three or four, or more, years in a row. That's when the fund's marketing machine kicks into high gear. We now have "the next Warren Buffett. He is managing our The Sky's the Limit growth fund, awarded 5-star status by Morningstar for 3 years in a row." Everyone and his uncle now pile into "The Sky's" high flying fund, certain that they have the right professional in charge of their hard earned money.

Unfortunately, just about the time everyone is in "The Sky's," and it actually does reach its limit, now it's more like "Limit Down" rather than "Limit Up." Why does this happen in almost every case of extraordinary early fund manager success, especially when looking at results for the succeeding ten-year period? Because there are very few fund managers (in spite of their higher intelligence, and education in most cases) with enough stock-picking skill to continue beating the market, year after year. Good luck with finding those few. You would need to wait at least 10 years to get some idea whether their success resulted from luck or skill at all.

Don't waste your time looking for an investment guru. If you really think about it, most of the time their tempo-rary success is indeed due to luck. Why is this so? Isn't this their chosen profession, one in which they supposedly spend so many weekly hours researching the market and individual stocks? Yes, this is all true. Their problem is, as stated earlier, that so are hundreds of other highly edu-cated, motivated, and intelligent professional stock pickers. All of these fund managers, in large part, 'are the market'; therefore, it is difficult for them to beat themselves, so to speak, on a long-term basis. And, most fund managers have a short-term bias anyway that hurts long-term results, because their jobs usually depend on getting results sooner rather than later.

You, by the way, as a long-term index fund investor following the SSA Strategy, have a big advantage over these "professionals." Why? Precisely because you will not get any redemption request pressures from impatient customers forcing you to sell their stock at a loss when you don't want to. Also because you are playing "the long game," unlike the "professional" fund manager under pressure to deliver results yesterday. And, finally, in terms of your asset allocation, all you need to do is match the market, not beat it, and you will—with the right index funds diversification. But, you ask, "I thought that your system shows me how I can beat the market." That's true. You will be able to beat the market over time by buying stock "on sale" during stock market corrections and crashes, and then waiting until that stock appreciates in value as the market retraces upward. Then following this with rebalancing within your portfolio as the rules dictate.

Your individual asset allocation is made up of the index funds and stock/bond-cash ratio you choose and plug into the SSA System. I'm saying that a diversified stock index fund combination will stand on its own in comparison to the results of the "professionals," even if the SSA System is not used. Additionally, why not just juice those market-matching returns with Strategic Stock Accumulation?

Since the vast majority of managed funds cannot beat the market over time, those lucky few that do, for possibly several years or more, then become subject to the law of 'reversion to the mean.' So now, all the newer investors in The Sky's the Limit fund become the victims of this law. In other words, if a fund manager is simply lucky for three years, he is more likely to also become unlucky for a number of years (law of averages). Unfortunately, this reversion most often exceeds the mean by declining below the mean, so that the next three or four years show below average stock market results. However, when all the six to eight years are taken together, the manager's results are usually close to the average (i.e. the mean) for all managed funds (unless the manager is worse than the average fund manager, in which case the results are even worse). More recently entering investors will have been unlucky enough to experience just the last three or four year's poor market results.

However, stock analysts, not brokers, and some economists who track and study entire industries and/or the stock market as a whole and give opinions on both, can serve an individual investor's purpose. The ulterior motive or agenda of this type of analyst is not the investor's money, but his or her reputation as an accurate market or industry forecaster. It's easier to forecast results for an entire industry than it is for individual stocks. This is for the same reason an index fund is better to invest in than are individual stocks. A market analyst is less likely to be wrong about most or all of the companies within an industry, than he or she is about an individual stock. I watch CNN Financial, for example, on most days for this type of researched market opinion, because it gives me information about industry sectors, or the market as a whole, of which I am always interested in. (You will not need all of this information to implement SSA).

Buying index funds only is not just my idea. The following well-known individuals, considered experts in the financial community, have all recommended the wisdom that echoes most investors using index funds:

Jack Bogle, founder of Vanguard, and known to be the "author of index investing".

Burton Malkiel, author of the classic work, *A Random Walk Down Wall Street*.

William Bernstein, author of *The Four Pillars of Investing*, and numerous other books on stock market investing.

Jack R. Meyer, former president of Harvard Management Company, who tripled the Harvard Investment Fund from $8 billion to $27 billion.

And finally, the most respected living long-term successful investor, Warren Buffett.

The above individuals have all made statements on record in no uncertain terms, in favor of stock index investing for most individuals. Due to copyright restrictions and the probable time required to grant permission for each quotation, I have not included specific statements. However, now enters the genius of the internet. You can simply search for any of the above names and add "stock index fund investing". You should be able to bring up not only specific statements, but even more important, the exact context in which they were made. The number of recognized financial professionals recommending stock index funds for most investors continues to grow unabated.

Investment managers' conflict of interest will not change until investors force the change!

So to use a golf analogy, try to avoid the temptation to shoot for eagles and even birdies. Just shooting par over for a long period of time (by capturing almost all of the total stock market's return through index funds), will make you more successful than the vast majority of investors—and even more so, when using index funds as part of the Strategic Stock Accumulation (SSA) Strategy described in this book.

Since 2005, the expense ratio of Vanguard's S&P 500 index fund has been .18%, and .09% for longer-term investors who were willing to invest $100,000 or more in the fund. Even these low costs have gone down. This fund now charges .05% expense ratio for all investors. The Vanguard Fund far outpaced the Wells Fargo Fund (another index fund), for example, during this period. This happened mainly because of the expense difference. There is no question that the lowest cost index funds are the most successful. Learn from this that all index funds are not the same in terms of costs; although, on average, they are much cheaper than managed funds.

It's important for investors to compare the costs involved with different index funds. This is very easy. Exchange-traded index funds have their expense ratios printed in their prospectuses and also online. So don't just pick the first stock index (or bond) fund that you come across. More of the larger discount brokerage houses are following Vanguard's lead and offering low expense ratio index funds. I like Vanguard, however, because it is truly a 'mutual' type of company owned by the investors, rather than a "for-profit." Think of it like Mutual of Omaha in the insurance industry. If a company doesn't need to make profits for private owners, then expenses ratios come down.

I sometimes explain to others that I am part owner of Vanguard as a part of personal disclosure. They, many times, think I am saying I own stock in the company. This is not true. There are no private stockholders of Vanguard. It is not a public or private company in the usual sense of either word. It truly is a 'mutual' company. Okay, so then, if I am part owner of Vanguard, how am I compensated for the company's success? I don't get a salary or any year-end bonus. So what do I get, besides good execution of buy and sell orders? I get paid in the form of continual lowered expense ratios. Instead of paying out profits to shareholders in the form of dividends, or even in capital appreciation of stock or by some other form of remuneration, I get continually lowered expense ratios (i.e., management fees).

The money which would be paid out to the private owners of xyz brokerage firm is not paid out by Vanguard but instead the management expenses charged investors are reduced by close to that same amount, which would otherwise be paid to the owners. There is some very minor management cost associated, however, even with index funds (after all, somebody in management has to look at the fund sometimes).

Every month, on Vanguard's website, the company lists expense ratio changes. The decreases far outnumber the increases. The few monthly expense ratio increases usually are associated with Vanguard's managed funds. They do have them, although their focus is on index funds. Yet even these managed funds have significantly lower expense ratios than the industry average.

As more investors continue to make the switch to brokerage firms focused on low-cost index funds, such as Vanguard, their costs continue to decrease. This is because, as they gain more customers, their costs are spread over an increasingly large base of investors. This is good for all investors. We can thank Vanguard for 'breaking the mold' on these expense ratios, as well as for the widespread industry acceptance of index funds in general.

CHAPTER 5: Several Better Known but Less Effective Stock Strategies

Dollar Cost Averaging

I want to give a short description of several non-SSA stock market investing strategies. This is mainly to help investors make a comparison with Strategic Stock Accumulation and also simply to acquaint him or her with the better known strategies, if not already known. Two of the strategies described in this chapter, Proportional Rebalancing and maintaining a 100% All-Stock Portfolio, are compared with SSA in Chapter 9 (on "Back-Testing Three Strategies" through six different time periods), so it is important to have a basic understanding of both strategies. Investors already knowledgeable about these strategies may appreciate reading along for a good review.

Dollar Cost Averaging has been around a long time. Basically, the idea is that you invest roughly the same amount of money in the stock market and usually at about the same periodic intervals. Some stock shares will be bought at higher prices and some at lower prices, but the idea is that since the overall trend of the stock market is up, more shares will be bought at lower prices. Over time, this effect will become more pronounced, and the investor's portfolio will gain accordingly. This sounds good. One criticism is that Dollar Cost Averaging is just a marketing gimmick that financial advisers use to ease worried investors into the stock market.

One pitch brokers give is that Dollar Cost Averaging reduces the risk of investing a one-time lump sum, should the investor consider doing so, just as the stock market may be due for a correction. It is advised to add partial amounts over time to the stock market, using Dollar Cost Averaging, instead of investing all at once. However, once all the money is in the market, it is 100% invested in stock. This causes a problem in that with Dollar Cost Averaging, the investor then takes on 100% market risk. This occurs when either investing a regular amount every month, or a lump sum at one time, and then regular monthly additional investments. One hundred percent (100%) of this money goes into stock (not into cash or bonds) in a typical Dollar Cost Averaging Strategy. You would typically be investing a fixed amount of dollars, every month or quarter, in the stock market.

The 100% stock market portfolio is only an acceptable idea when the investor is young to middle-aged. It is a bad idea for an older individual right before or during retirement, because there may not be enough time left to recuperate financially from a market crash or severe correction. Many 401(k)s and IRAs are invested in this manner. What can be said positively for this method is that if followed consistently, Dollar Cost Averaging is a good way to encourage regular savings into an investment account. If followed over many years, it will most likely result in positive asset accumulation.

Unfortunately, if the stock market is experiencing a long period of time in overvaluation mode, many more shares will be bought that are also overvalued. On the other hand, when the market becomes undervalued, shares are indeed purchased at a lower price, but there is definitely a better strategy to accumulate stock that is undervalued. That better way is the Strategic Stock Accumulation Strategy, as explained in Chapter 8.

Value Averaging

Michael Edleson devised a system that he termed, Value Averaging, back in the early 1990s. He was then an assistant professor at the Harvard Business School. The basic concept of Value Averaging is similar to Dollar Cost Averaging in the sense that additions to a stock portfolio are made on a regular (in this case, monthly) basis. It is different than Dollar Cost Averaging in the sense that, in addition to investing a regular sum of money over time, the amount invested monthly is based on a specific formula.

Value Averaging requires an investor to first determine how much money he or she needs to accumulate in order to reach a future goal, such as retirement. The investor then tries to determine what the expected return will be in the stock market on average each year until retirement. Then, he or she should be able to determine, by working backwards, how much is needed to invest each month to reach the final goal.

If the goal, for example, is a $1 million portfolio in 20 years, and the investor is starting with zero dollars in the account, he or she might make the following assumptions: The stock market has returned very close to 10% on a nominal basis on average over many years. Nominal means including inflation. If we subtract the average 3% to 4% inflation rate over the last 30-40 years, give or take a half a percent, then the real return over that period is closer to 6 1/2%. If the investor is conservative and assumes an 8% nominal (inflation added) return, then he or she needs to save $1,750 each month. Progress can then be checked each month to see if everything is on track for this goal. If at the end of two years, 2 months, there is $50,000 when there should be $51, 600, then this represents a $1,600 shortfall. So, according to the Value Averaging Strategy, the investor must invest an additional $1,600 the next month to stay on track. This process would be repeated each month thereafter, and in months when there was a shortfall, extra money would have to be invested to get back on track. In those months where the stock market increased to the point it represented a dollar figure over the monthly goal, then less money, or maybe none, would need to be invested.

The advantage of this strategy over Dollar Cost Averaging is that it is more predictably systematic. Monthly dollar analysis of the portfolio allows an investor to know exact amounts and whether or not the investment is on track toward the goal. Of course, this assumes that the investor is right in his or her prediction of what the stock market returns will be over the next 20 years (and more importantly, what the individual return will be), which will always actually be questionable. Assuming the investor is correct, then what needs to be done is always known when the monthly dollar figure is not on track.

The main drawback of this strategy is the difficulty of following it during a prolonged slump in the stock market. If a prolonged severe (or even moderate) bear market occurs, an investor could be required to make monthly contributions beyond his or her financial capability just to stay on track. Another serious drawback of this strategy is that it is really no stock market strategy at all! It tells the investor nothing whatsoever about how to invest his money (i.e., the types of stocks and bonds, what percentages, how often to sell or rebalance, if ever, what asset allocation— nothing about any of this is mentioned!) The strategy just tells the investor to choose a return and plan on it. Also, the monthly dollar investment amounts required during bear markets could triple or quadruple, likely forcing the investor to discontinue this strategy.

If the stock market is experiencing a roaring bull market, and the profits on paper reduce or eliminate the necessity of monthly stock purchases during that time, the investor may get used to investing little or nothing each month and find it difficult, budget-wise, to begin making large contributions again when the inevitable stock market reversal occurs.

This strategy can also require a significant amount of time investment—time many investors would not wish to continue "investing" in, especially if they are forced to continue adding larger amounts of money monthly into a declining stock market. The Value Averaging Strategy does, indeed, offer a way to continue adding to an investment account, if followed. This strategy is fairly well-known among many investment advisers; however, as a practical strategy, not many investors seem to be following it, probably for the reasons mentioned above.

Proportional Rebalancing

In Chapter 8, I will lay out the Strategic Stock Accumulation Strategy and also compare this strategy (Chapter 9) by back-testing, with probably the two most common methods used today by most investors who follow any strategy at all. Those two strategies are Proportional Rebalancing and a 100% All-Stock portfolio (the "no brainer" strategy). There are pros and cons associated with both of these strategies. In comparison with Strategic Stock Accumulation, the cons of these other two strategies outweigh the pros.

Under Proportional Rebalancing, an initial asset allocation is set up, for example, 50% stock and 50% bonds and/or cash, or a 50/50 stock/bonds-cash ratio. Asset Allocation is explained in more detail in the next chapter. For purposes of this example, just think of the portfolio as consisting of half stock and half bonds (and/or cash). At the end of a predetermined interval, for example, one year, the portfolio is rebalanced to reestablish the initial 50/50 stock/bonds-cash ratio. If the stock portion of the portfolio has gained in value and now represents 60% of the portfolio, then enough index fund stock shares would be sold to reestablish the beginning ratio. On the other hand, if the stock portion lost value over the year, then enough of the bond and/or cash part of the portfolio would be sold to purchase stock at end of the year, thereby reestablishing the 50/50 stock/bond-cash ratio. You can see how Proportional Rebalancing forces an investor to buy stock at lower prices and sell higher. Many investment managers today refer to Proportional Rebalancing as simply asset allocation and (periodic) rebalancing (usually once per year).

The two main drawbacks of this strategy are that first: In a roaring bull market, large amounts of stock may be sold at the end of the year when the stock market is still making large gains, resulting in reduced profits; and second: In a moderate or severe bear market, the specific PR Rebalancing Strategy does not allow for sufficient buying of stock "on sale," as I'll explain in much more detail in the next several chapters.

100% All-Stock Portfolio

Surprisingly, the 100% All-Stock Strategy (i.e., at all times) is not a bad one for a young investor, and probably not bad up to late middle age either, contrary to much investment advice today. The fear, of course among many, is that an all-stock portfolio exposes the investor to too much risk, especially during a market crash or severe correction.

Most financial advisers advocate a more "balanced portfolio" that includes stocks, bonds, and cash. Many investment managers today like to talk about how every investor needs to have individualized financial goals, based upon his or her own financial situation (with the help of one of these financial "advisers," of course!) I've already talked about my views on those "professionals."

If an investor absolutely does not want to be involved with buy/sell decisions for his portfolio, or just lacks the self-confidence to do so, then yes, definitely hire a financial adviser. Just keep this in mind: Your goal is to make money, just like everyone else investing in the stock and bond markets. The "help" of an adviser will cost you money. Over an investment lifetime, this will subtract many dollars from an investment account. There is a much better and less expensive way to accumulate assets for retirement or any other long-term goal. That is by buying index funds and using them within the Strategic Stock Accumulation Strategy. Knowledge is power. The more investment knowledge you have, the more power and confidence you will possess in your investment decisions. So, give yourself a chance. Don't automatically succumb to the fear generated by the investment industry. You can learn to make your own investment decisions without the expensive "help" of an investment adviser. You can put your investment program on "automatic pilot" until year-end, with you in the driver's seat by implementing SSA.

If you are concerned in any way about the risks of the Strategic Stock Accumulation strategy, then by all means, get it evaluated by a financial adviser, or your accountant. It is important to understand, as will be fully explained in Chapter 8, that since you will be buying stock as the stock market declines, as part of the SSA strategy, your portfolio will obviously show a decrease in value until the stock market retraces back to its pre-crash level. If the stock market declines close to, or exceeds the historical crash average of over 50%, this decline will be very significant. That is, until this stock market retracement to pre-crash levels takes place. Then, assuming you followed the Strategic Stock Accumulation strategy, your profits will be very significant, well over and above any paper losses from the stock market crash or correction.

I don't deny that you should set up your initial asset allocation based, to a large extent, on your age. And, to the extent that your age is different from the investor down the street, your stock/bond-cash allocation should be different too. But it doesn't take a "professional" to figure this out, especially if he or she is taking 1% or more, per year, from you to do it. I'll explain how to do it, based on your age, for free (except for the cost of this book) in Chapter 7, "Choosing Your Stock/Bond-Cash Ratio."

Interestingly enough, when the stock market is going "great guns," there is always talk about the importance of being a "long-term investor." This is code for "I'm fully invested (100% stock) right now, and I'm not going to miss any of this bull market by being only partially invested in stock—I'm 'all in.' I'm not worried about a temporary drop in the stock market. I'm a long-term investor. Besides, it always comes back, right?" This was certainly the prevailing market wisdom up to the Spring of 2000, just before that market crash.

I'm not totally opposed to a 100% All-Stock (AS) Strategy (although SSA is much better) if, and this is a big IF, the investor is not older and retired. Also, if he or she were foolish enough to be 100% invested in stock, this investor would then be in a very precarious position if the stock market were to drop very quickly. If this investor sells out on the way down, the profits are permanently lost from the move back up as the market recovers. If the investor holds his or her position and doesn't sell, then he or she runs the risk of being invested in a prolonged bear market. Can this investor handle the situation psychologically as well as financially? Maybe, maybe not. But why take the risk at that age?

Now, in 2014, investors are more cautious. But, according to the latest brokerage house figures, the stock percentage of the average portfolio continues to increase, in spite of the stock market continuing to hit new highs now (i.e., as of July, 2014).

So, what's the story? Is it really true that a younger investor could do much worse than staying 100% invested in stock at all times? The answer that I found in back-testing this strategy to 1972 (41 years) surprised me. It is true, as I'll show in Chapter 9: a 100% All-Stock portfolio did much better than the Proportional Rebalancing Strategy. It did, however, lag behind the SSA Strategy at all three tested stock/bond-cash ratios. I assumed that such a portfolio would take too many years for many investors to make up the losses incurred during those two severe stock market crashes of 2000 and 2008–2009. I guess, however, that this depends on how you define "too many years." The stock market had recovered its lost ground in both of those crashes within three to four years.

Tens of thousands of All-Stock Strategy investors lost from 40 to 60% of their portfolio and total net worth twice! However, when the entire 41-year period (to 2013 year-end) is taken into account, the results of this strategy are much different, as is documented in Chapter 9.

The obvious drawback of this strategy is that for rela-tively long periods of time, the stock market can stay in bear market mode. Many investors lose patience and become fearful, causing them to sell, missing forever the succeeding retracement of the market. When the stock market eventually does reach its previous high again (and beyond), the profits that should have resulted are gone because of panic selling on the way down. This widespread investor reluctance to "stay the course" during a severe stock market downturn is quite likely the reason for the poor reputation of the All-Stock Strategy. It does make sense for an older or retired investor, if he or she is 100% in stock, to sell out quickly from such a portfolio at the first credible sign of a market turn. But, older and retired investors should never be involved with this strategy to begin with.

CHAPTER 6: Choosing the Index Funds for Your Asset Allocation

First, let me emphasize the Strategic Stock Accumulation Strategy can be started, and an initial asset allocation set up, ANY time of the year, not just year-end. Don't wait until year-end to start buying your initial grouping of index funds to get started. After your particular asset allocation is set up, from that point on you need to wait until calendar year-end to buy, according to the "Buy Rules".

Asset Allocation simply refers to the way in which the assets within your investment account are set up. There are two parts to your asset allocation: the stock part (index funds) and the bond-cash part (U.S. Treasury inflation protected bonds, short-term U.S. bond funds and money market funds). You can start the SSA Strategy with less than $10,000, but that amount or more will be a better initial investment. Under that amount, I suggest concentrating on saving enough money (Chapter 2) to get that initial $10,000.

If you have only $10,000 to $25,000 to invest initially, then there will be a problem buying ten to twelve stock and bond index funds as listed in Charts 1 and 2. This is because Vanguard, as do most discount brokerage firms, requires a minimum of $2,500 to $3000 per initial investment in EACH fund. In the case of Vanguard, this would mean an investor would need at least $30,000 (10 times $3000) to fully fund an initial investment in the SSA Strategy using Chart 2, for example.

So, let's look at how such a situation could be handled, so that an investor could still begin the SSA Strategy with this lower initial balance. If he or she has only $10,000 total, for example, to invest initially in SSA, and is beginning the strategy with a 65/35 Stock/Bond-Cash Ratio, then he or she would allocate (divide up) the $10,000 in the following manner. Simply invest in only two stock funds (in the stock portion) and one money market fund (in the bond-cash portion) to begin the strategy. $3,300 should be invested in an S&P 500 index fund, and $3,200 invested in a small-cap index fund, such as a Russell 2000 small-cap index fund. These two purchases would represent 65% of the $10,000 ($6,500) of the portfolio. Then put the remaining $3,500 (35% of $10,000) into a money market fund. This MMF would be in the bond-cash portion of the portfolio. All discount brokerage firms have money market funds available to "sweep" money into, from stock and bond sales. There won't be enough money left to buy any other stock or bond funds at this point.

As the portfolio increases over time through asset appreciation and investor added funds, he or she would simply buy more of the listed index funds in Charts 1 or 2 in $3,000 increments. The investor will need to sell parts of some of the other funds which have appreciated in value to accomplish this. The simple way to do this is to add up all portfolio value over $3,000 in each presently owned fund. Then sell those funds down to $3,000. Use these additional dollars to buy another fund once this additional total reaches $3,000. For example, if the S&P 500 fund, a year later, is worth $4,800, and the Russell 2000 small-cap index fund is now at $4,700, then sell parts of both of those funds, so that they are both again

worth only $3,000 each. Then use the $3000 total proceeds ($9,500 minus $6,500 equals $3,000) from these
two stock index sales to buy another fund in either Chart 1
or 2. Repeat this process until all funds in either Charts 1 or
2 are part of the portfolio. While slowly adding these additional funds, follow all other SSA rules, including year-end
internal rebalancing (This is explained in detail in Chapter
8). Use the same directions described above to start SSA
with any beginning dollar amount between $10,000 and
$32,900. Obviously it is better to start the strategy with at
least $33,000. Eventually, the investor will be able
to incorporate all listed index funds in either Chart 1 or 2
by following the above described procedure. When at least
$33,000 is available for investment in SSA, begin the
strategy as described below.

First, determine which specific stock index funds you
wish to include in the stock portion of your portfolio. You
will do this by choosing either the funds in Asset Allocation
1 or 2. You will have 8 or 10 different index funds in each to
choose from (see Charts 1 and 2). This may seem excessive,
and that it would require a large time commitment. But,
once the funds are chosen (by choosing either Chart 1 or 2)
and included in the portfolio, they only need to be checked
for possible additional purchases or sales, in most cases,
once a year (there is one exception to this once a year rule,
as will be explained in chapter 8). You must choose which
actual funds to buy, and make sure that they are, as much
as possible, close to the kinds of funds listed in each Asset
Allocation (Chart 1 or 2). Simply choose the funds closest to
the ones listed on Chart 1 or 2, from the stock index fund
categories within your discount brokerage list of available
funds. If not sure about this, have a brokerage representative walk you through this process. They should be more
than happy to do this.

Both Charts 1 and 2 start with an assumed initial
$100,000 investment. That amount, as stated above, is cer-
tainly not necessary to start. It is only used as a round
figure example. Whatever your initial investment in your
use of the SSA Strategy, simply take that percentage of
$100,000 and calculate all of your figures from that per-

centage.

You may be wondering, "Why can't I just pick my own type of different index funds and have fewer (or more) than shown in Charts 1 or 2?" You certainly have that right, but then you are not really following SSA, and it's harder to predict the long-term results.

The actual percentage each stock fund (and bond fund) that will, in total, comprise your portfolio will depend upon the stock/bond-cash ratio you are using. How that is determined will be explained fully in the next chapter. These ratios are also included in Asset Allocation Charts 1 and 2.

CHARTS 1 and 2: $100,000 Portfolio

CHART1
$100,000 PORTFOLIO SSA

Asset Allocation Portfolio

Stock Index Funds

	65%	50%	35%
S&P 500 Index Fund	6.5	5.0	3.5
US Small Cap Index Fund	6.5	5.0	3.5
US Mid-Cap Index Fund	6.5	5.0	3.5
Large Technology Index Fund	6.5	5.0	3.5
Real Estate Investment Trust Index Fund (REIT)	6.5	5.0	3.5
Precious Metals Index Fund	6.5	5.0	3.5
International Markets Index Fund	6.5	5.0	3.5
Europe Index Fund	6.5	5.0	3.5
Developing Markets Index Fund	6.5	5.0	3.5
Emerging Markets Index Fund			
Totals	65%	50%	35%

Bonds-Cash Index Funds

	35%	50%	65%
Short-Term US Treasury Inflation Protected Bonds Fund	7	10	13
Short-Term US Govt Bond Fund	14	20	26
Money Market Fund	14	20	26
Totals	35%	50%	65%

CHART2
$100,000 PORTFOLIO SSA

Asset Allocation Portfolio	Stock Index Funds				Bonds-Cash Index Funds		
	65%	50%	35%		35%	50%	65%
S&P 500 Index Fund	8.3	6.3	4.4	Short-Term US Treasury Inflation Protected Bonds Fund	7	10	13
US Small Cap Index Fund	8.1	6.3	4.4	Short-Term US Govt Bond Fund	14	20	26
US Mid-Cap Index Fund	8.1	6.3	4.4	Money Market Fund	14	20	26
Large Technology Index Fund	8.1	6.3	4.4				
International Markets Index Fund	8.1	6.2	4.35				
Europe Index Fund	8.1	6.2	4.35				
Developing Markets Index Fund	8.1	6.2	4.35				
Emerging Markets Index Fund	8.1	6.2	4.35				
TOTALS	65%	50%	35%		35%	50%	65%

At this point, you are only deciding which stock index funds to buy within your asset allocation, by choosing those funds of the asset allocation within Chart 1 or Chart 2. There are several important reasons to have at least eight stock funds (Chart 2) within this part of your portfolio, as I will discuss in more detail later in this chapter.

You will need to open a discount brokerage account with a firm such as Vanguard or Fidelity. Don't go with a so-called full service brokerage firm, as their fees, by and large, are much higher. Vanguard probably has the lowest expense ratios in the discount brokerage industry, although the other discount brokerage firms have been forced by Vanguard to follow suit, to some extent, in order to remain competitive. Their problem is that they must make a profit for their company's owners, whereas Vanguard does not.

Vanguard is a mutual-type brokerage firm with a unique corporate structure. Any profits are given back to the customers (possibly you) in the form of lower expense ratios. At any rate, choose one. You can then include all of your stock, bond, and cash assets within the brokerage firm and easily switch between stocks, bonds, and cash, as the need arises. You want to be able to switch between bonds (and cash) and stock quickly, as the Buy and Sell Rules of SSA are triggered.

Within the bond-cash portion of your portfolio, you will include a Treasury inflation-protected securities (TIPS) fund, a short-term U. S. bond fund, and a money market fund, in the percentages shown in either Chart 1 or 2. The actual percentage owned of each bond in your total portfolio will depend on your stock/bond-cash ratio, the same as with the stock portion. This stock/bond-cash ratio choice will be fully explained in the next chapter: "determining your Stock/Bond-Cash Ratio.

"You will move money in and out of these index funds according to the 'buy/sell' Rules of Charts 3 and 4. During any annual rebalancing of the portfolio, these original bond-cash percentages would also be reestablished in the same manner, as for the stock portion. It is only the individual funds that are rebalanced routinely every year-end (back to their equal stock percentages in charts 1 or 2), not the overall stock/bond-cash ratio. Rebalancing of the entire stock/bond-cash ratio occurs only when the 'sell' rules are triggered. I will explain this in more detail in chapter 8.

There are 10 stock index funds that make up the asset allocation of Chart 1. Why these particular index funds? Our goal is to cover as much of the world stock market as possible, not just the U.S. market. Why is this important? Because the U.S. stock market no longer dominates the world as it once did. Europe's economic activity is comparable to the U.S., and Asia is growing faster than all other areas of the world. If one or two of these world regions stagnate, and this stagnation is reflected in their stock markets, it is certainly possible that one or two of the other regions will buck the trend and do the opposite. So, by being invested in all areas of the world, we can take advantage of the timing differential through the process of rebalancing.

Chart 1 is made up of five U.S. index funds, four international index funds, and a precious metals fund. The five U.S. funds cover large-capitalization, mid-capitalization, and small-capitalization corporations, as well as a real estate investment trust, so it is well diversified. Likewise, the international index funds include the larger developed markets and also emerging markets. All 10 stock index funds are given equal weight in dollar and percentage terms, so that when rebalancing occurs, the equal weighting is reestablished. The important point to remember is that there may be relatively long periods of time when several or more of the funds outperform other funds in the group. It is vitally important not to give up on the laggards and sell any of them. That would defeat the whole benefit of rebalancing. It is the process of buying lower and selling higher within the fund group that rebalancing forces the investor to do. That is what is responsible for the additional return of SSA over and above the return of the larger basic SSA strategy itself. So, when a fund is lagging, keep in mind that this fund is not like an individual stock that may be in danger of possible bankruptcy. Index funds are comprised of a large group of stocks that will on average, ultimately return to profitability. The farther down that fund lags, the greater the potential future profit as you buy more through the rebalancing process.

During the rebalancing process, you would sell those funds that have outperformed other funds within the portfolio. You also would buy more of those stock funds that have lagged the others. How do you know how much of these different stock funds to buy and sell? That's easy. You simply buy and sell to the extent that you are able to reestablish your original stock percentages within the stock portion of your portfolio.

For example, if you started with $50,000 in the stock portion of your portfolio ($100,000 total in a 50/50 stock/bond-cash ratio total portfolio), and at the end of year one, you had $60,000 in this part of the portfolio (because your stock gained 20% for the year), you would then divide the total $60,000 evenly among all 10 stock index funds for $6,000 in each fund. You would then buy and sell the index funds within the stock portion of your portfolio to reflect these new individual stock index fund values. This would force you to buy lower and sell higher.

This rebalancing should take place at least once every year. If you are buying stock as a result of a stock market crash, then you would buy the same way to reestablish the original equal percentages within the stock part of the portfolio. Any stock purchase or sale, as a result of the other 'buy' or 'sell' rules would count toward this one-year rebalancing rule. Just remember, you will <u>not</u> change the <u>overall</u> stock/bond ratio back to the original percentages, until it is indicated to do so by the "Sell Rules" of Chart 4. Intuitively, as well as rationally, we can see that this positive rebalancing effect will be significant over the years.

Chart 1 shows the asset allocation with 10 stock funds. Chart 2 shows an asset allocation with eight index stock funds in it. The stock index funds making up Chart 2 are the same as in Chart 1, except for the deletion of the Real Estate Investment Trust and the Precious Metals fund (as some investors may have philosophical or other objections to one or both of these categories). Both of these charts are excellent models for the SSA Strategy. The first stock asset allocation (Chart 1) should allow for a slightly larger rebalancing advantage over time. You can decide which discount brokerage firm to buy the individual index funds from, although I would look closely at the expense ratio of each fund. They can differ significantly, even though on average, they are lower than managed funds. You can look this up online, or in the fund's prospectus. The prospectus for each fund is required by law and gives the relevant financial information about the fund.

Both stock portfolios would require a time commitment only a few weeks or so before year-end, with one exception, which I'll explain later. Most investors will spend time checking on their portfolio during the year. That's certainly ok, but in most cases I would wait until year-end to make any buy/sell changes. This makes it much easier to follow the SSA Strategy, but more important, allows the investor to more closely follow the long-term secular trends of the stock market. By this, I mean that it is possible for an investor to use up his or her cash faster (to buy stock) if this is done before waiting until year-end. If waiting until year-end during a longer-term bear market, stock may very well be available at even lower prices. It is true that a temporary drop in the stock market may be missed during the year, but on balance, I believe it's better to wait.

A little extra time devoted to any buying, selling, and/or rebalancing within the portfolio will be well worth it. I have included the slightly smaller stock portfolio (8 funds instead of 10) for those investors wanting something slightly simpler. The other reason for this second asset allocation (Chart 2), as stated above, is that that it does not include a precious metals index fund or real estate investment trust index fund, as does Chart 1. Some investors may not wish to invest in these two types of investments, believing that they are not really stocks or reflective of the stock market as a whole. They are both owned with a corporate stock structure, so I see no problem with including them. Also, they provide some greater diversification and lower portfolio correlation, but you can decide that for yourself.

The two portfolios include stocks, bonds, and cash. The benefits of a somewhat larger and more diversified asset allocation (as compared to some other investment strategies) are significant within the SSA Strategy. Both examples (Charts 1 and 2) will deliver more than adequate diversification and stock market return potential. Again, the asset allocation with 10 funds in it, assuming SSA is followed correctly, should return a slightly higher future figure, because of the rebalancing potential offered with those added metals and real estate funds. However, if this slightly higher time requirement is not provided for, in terms of year-end rebalancing, the additional funds in the asset allocation will probably provide no added benefit. Just remember, you will need to watch all of them prior to year-end, regardless. Short-term U.S. bonds, and TIPS, as well as cash, are the best choices for the bond-cash portion of your portfolio, because they give the best interest rate (though pathetically small at this time), taking into consideration duration (time) risk. "duration risk" is referring to the time risk of inflation; a short-term duration is a lot less risky than a longer-term duration to worry about inflation ravaging the value of your bonds. Also, there is an increased chance of taking a larger capital loss with longer-term bonds when converting them to cash. Remember, bonds lose value as interest rates rise, and the longer the duration of the bond, the greater the risk.

It is also true that if the stock market crashes quickly, the Federal Reserve is likely to lower interest rates, at least in the short run, in order to help provide quick liquidity to the market and economy. This could actually give you a profit on your bonds, as you sell to convert the bonds to cash, since this Fed activity will have the interest lowering effect it desires. However, if the stock market is slowly declining or if rising inflation is a threat, then the Fed is less likely to lower rates, unless it fears a recession. Regardless, you will be selling your bonds, converting to cash, and then purchasing stock index funds during the next market correction or crash.

Once you decide on Asset Allocation Chart 1 or 2 for your portfolio, you will then be able to "plug in" the stock portion of your asset allocation into one of the three stock/bond-cash ratios appropriate to your age in the SSA

Strategy. The three ratios again are: 65/35 (stock/bonds-cash), 50/50 (stock/bonds-cash), and 35/65 (stock/bonds-cash). These ratios are all included in both asset allocations of Charts 1 and 2. This will be explained in the next chapter.

The asset allocation decision (Chart 1 or 2), will determine **which stocks** to include in one part of the portfolio, and **which bonds-cash** to include in the other part, **as well as which stock/bond-cash ratio to use. How much of each stock fund (in dollar terms) compared to bonds and cash** to include in your portfolio makes up the stock/bond-cash ratio decision. **These are both primary decisions**. The **type** of index funds to actually include in the portfolio is the first part of any asset allocation decision and will be decided by choosing either asset allocation in Chart 1 or 2. The stock/bond-cash ratio decision is the second part of the asset allocation decision. The three stock/bond-cash ratio options are also shown on charts 1 and 2.

Asset Allocation Charts 1 and 2 include the three stock/bond-cash ratio options, as well as the percentage breakdown of each index fund within the asset allocation. Again, this is the second important asset allocation decision, and will be explained in the next chapter.

Diversification within your portfolio is vitally important. Diversification can be described as "not putting all of your eggs in one basket." Within the stock market, there are two different types of risk: individual stock risk, which I have talked about in a previous chapter (the kind that you will avoid completely by buying only index funds), and market risk, which is the risk of a correction or crash occurring in the stock market as a whole. The primary goal of all mutual funds, including index funds, is the avoidance of individual stock risk through diversification. An investor can diversify even beyond a single mutual or index fund by investing in multiple funds in different industries, markets or countries, and with different market correlations.

Harry Markowitz, Nobel Laureate, developed Modern Portfolio Theory that quantifies the benefits of diversification. This was not research on a stock market investing

strategy beyond the description of research on the importance of diversification and correlation. Markowitz
emphasized the importance of all assets (including stock)
within a portfolio being set up so that all of its components
together are situated on what he called "the efficient frontier." The efficient frontier is that combination of individual
investments that, when taken together, result in the
greatest return for the amount of risk taken. Or, another
way to say it is: The efficient frontier is the least amount of
risk taken for any combination of portfolio assets. To
accomplish this portfolio goal, the investor needs to choose
stocks and bonds that include, not only sufficient diversification, but also have sufficiently low correlation between
those assets.

Diversification means including stocks and bonds
within the portfolio that are in different industries, of different sizes, and also in different countries. The reason for
this variety of stocks and bonds is that one or more industries, countries, or even stock size, frequently becomes out
of favor among investors and will decline in price as a
result. For whatever reason, there will be other assets in the
portfolio not so affected to counter this effect, possibly even
gaining in value.

"Correlation" refers to the tendency of one asset to gain
in value in relation to another. Two assets are said to be
correlated (or positively correlated) if they are both affected
the same way by market conditions. In other words, both
assets would probably go up or down at the same time.
Negatively correlated assets will tend to be affected differ-
ently by market forces. So, it is important to have adequate
diversification, as well as negatively correlated assets
within a portfolio.

When rebalancing is performed, this negative correlation
and diversification means that some assets will require larger
additional purchases and others less, while some will actually
be partially sold so that initial stock and bond percentages
can be correctly reestablished. The effect of this periodic
rebalancing really does represent a "free lunch," as the
investor buys more of the resulting lower priced stock funds
and sells part of the funds that rose in value to reestablish the

initial ratio. This rebalancing will occur at year-end within the SSA Strategy, assuming no Buy/Sell Rules have also been triggered at that time. If either of the 'buy' or 'sell' rules are triggered, you would not rebalance within your portfolio at that year-end, as this would already be accomplished by implementation of either the Buy or Sell Rules in Chart 5 (Chapter 8).

With little or no research required, the SSA investor can reap the rewards of an overall portfolio gain in value, through this annual rebalancing. This increase in value is over and above any increase in the value of the stock market. The SSA investor accomplishes this by simply buying, at lower prices, those stocks lagging others within the portfolio. He or she also sells, at higher prices, part of those index funds that have gained in value. This gain is also over and above the greater profit potential within the more profitable Buy/Sell Pyramid SSA Strategy, which is described in detail in Chapter 8. Chapter 8 will show how substantial profits are made as a result of additional stock bought "on sale" during stock market corrections and crashes. Those profits are realized down the road, as the sell rules are triggered.

The SSA investor following either asset allocation models of Charts 1 or 2 does not need to be concerned about diversification and correlation within the portfolio. Both of those asset allocations provide a more than adequate amount of each.

One final caveat: It's important to have at least 3-6 months of emergency funds separate from your dollars invested in SSA. I can't emphasize this strongly enough. You don't want to be in a position in which you are forced to sell part of the assets in your portfolio at or near the bottom of the stock market as a crash proceeds in order to cover an emergency or any unexpected expenses. This is even more important for retirees. At least 8 years (preferably 10) worth of living expenses should be provided for (include social security in this calculation). Treasury Inflation Protected Securities (TIPS) are an excellent way to get this covered. These funds are also a part of the bond-cash portion of Charts 1 and 2.

If an investor had \$25,000 invested in TIPS in the year 2000, for example, its purchasing power, even if it had a 0% interest yield for 10 years, would still have the same purchasing power (\$25,000) it had in year 2000—14 years later! These bonds are adjusted for inflation quarterly to reflect price changes due to inflation. The principal value of the bonds is adjusted this way, not the interest. This is based on the consumer price index (CPI). This is important for retirees, especially, who are always concerned about inflation eating away their savings. You may be concerned about the accuracy of the CPI figures used to calculate changes in the value of the TIPS. Don't be. The U.S. government knows that if they play around with these figures, minimizing the true rate of inflation, investors will soon figure this out and demand a higher rate of interest or no one will buy the bonds. This will needlessly cost the U.S. Treasury even more money.

CHAPTER 7: Determining Your Stock/Bond Cash Ratio

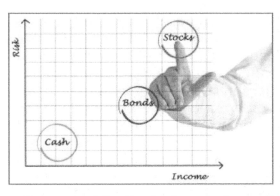

After choosing the stock and bond funds within your asset allocation (Chart 1 or 2), it is now time to determine your stock/bond-cash ratio. This involves determining what percentages will be represented by both the stock portion and the bond-cash portion of your portfolio. This decision will result in your own particular stock/bond-cash ratio.

Here is how you determine this ratio according to the SSA Strategy:

AGE: INVESTMENT LIFE START POINT TO AGE 40
65/35 STOCK/BOND-CASH RATIO
AGE: 41—55
50/50 STOCK/BOND-CASH RATIO
AGE: 56—INVESTMENT LIFE ENDPOINT
35/65 STOCK/BOND-CASH RATIO

So, for example, a 65/35 ratio means that 65% of the portfolio would be represented by stock index funds. And that 65% would be evenly divided among the stock funds in either Asset Allocation Chart 1 or 2. The 35% of the total assets would be in the bond-cash portion, and that would be divided according to the percentages also in Charts 1 or 2.

So, let's say an investor started with a $100,000 portfolio, a 65/35 stock/bond-cash ratio, and a Chart 1 Asset Allocation (see Chart 1-Asset Allocation Portfolio). ($100,000 is only used as an example. An investor could just as easily begin the SSA Strategy with $33,000 or even less and receive the same percentage results).

Following Chart 1, he or she would divide $65,000 evenly between all 10 stock index funds (6.5% each). The remaining $35,000 would then be allocated to the bond-cash portion of Chart 1 in the percentages indicated: Short-Term U.S. Treasury Inflation Protected Securities (TIPS)—7%, Short-Term U.S. Government Bond Fund—14%, and U.S. Money Market Fund—14%. The same process would be followed for 50/50 and 35/65 stock/bond-cash ratios, except that the percentages in each portion of those portfolios would reflect those different ratios. For example: if the 35/65 stock/bond-cash ratio is chosen along with the Chart 2 Asset Allocation Portfolio, then four of the stock index funds would comprise 4.4% of the overall portfolio, and the other four stock index funds would each have 4.35% of the total portfolio dollar value (see Chart 2, Asset Allocation Portfolio). You would also follow the cash-bond percentages listed within that particular asset allocation chart and ratio.

You will notice the above age range ratios indicate a higher stock percentage present in the portfolio when the investor is younger (65/35), and that this stock percentage decreases as he or she ages. The reason for this percentage change as time goes by is fairly obvious. The investor can live with higher stock risk when young, since there is a lot of time to bounce back from any crash or severe correction. Also, at this point in life, the investor is able to take greater advantage of the long-term upward march of the stock market. At middle age (41–55), the ratio becomes 50/50 stock/bond-cash to reflect his decreasing number of investment years. During an investor's final years, he would typically want the least amount of risk, even within the lower-risk SSA Strategy.

Now, having said the above, middle-aged, older, and/or retired investors can still reap large profits with their respective ratios. Over the 41-year period back-tested (Chapter 9), the 65/35 stock/bond-cash ratio performed best of all strategies and all ratios (Chart 9, Column 2, 1972–2013). Its cumulative return (CR) over the 41-year period was 883%, inflation-adjusted. So, why don't I just recommend this ratio for middle-age investors too? One reason is that intuitively, the 50/50 ratio is still able to take advantage of the lifetime rebalancing advantage within SSA and also allow for slightly less risk than 65/35 stock/bond-cash ratio portfolio (although the 65/35 SSA portfolio is much less risky than the 100% All-Stock Portfolio, for example). I was not able to back-test for the internal (within the portfolio) rebalancing effect of SSA. So that additional SSA return was not even included in the greater final 41-year stock market returns of Strategic Stock Accumulation Strategy.

I could only test the historical S&P values, and not the 8 to 10 stock index funds in a hypothetical investor's portfolio for the rebalancing advantage. This will definitely juice the final returns of the SSA Strategy.

Once you have chosen the stocks of either Chart 1 or 2 and determined your stock/bond-cash ratio within it, you can then plug in the stock index funds to your stock/bond-cash ratio within the Asset Allocation Chart of your choice. This is a simple matter of buying the stock index funds, and bond and cash funds in Chart 1 or 2, in the same ratio as your chosen stock/bond-cash ratio, as explained above. For example, a Chart 1 Asset Allocation portfolio with a 50/50 stock/bond-cash ratio, would have all 10 of the stock index funds allocated in the portfolio at 5% (see Chart 1, Column 3). The bond funds would be allocated at 10%, 20%, and 20% (Chart 1, Column 7). Once this is done, all you need to learn is how and when to buy and sell the stock and bond index funds within your chosen stock/bond-cash ratio portfolio. That is the subject of the next chapter.

You are now ready to learn how to implement the

Strategic Stock Accumulation Strategy, step by step, as will be described in Chapter 8.

CHAPTER 8: Strategic Stock Accumulation (SSA): The Strategy, Step by Step

The Strategic Stock Accumulation Strategy, or **SSA**, allows the investor to accumulate large amounts of stock strategically as the stock market drops during a severe market correction or crash. The name serves as an anchor to associate mentally with the strategic as well as the accumulative aspect of the strategy. It is based on a deliberate rules-based strategy. The strategy will act independent of any emotional or "the market is cheap now, so I should probably buy" type of mental guesswork.

Tax-wise, the SSA Strategy is very beneficial to the investor. As will be shown in the tables documenting these results, if an investor used the Strategic Stock Accumulation Strategy over a 41-year period (from 1972 to 2013), he or she, aside from internal rebalancing, would only have sold stock twice over that entire period! This means that outside of a tax-sheltered vehicle such as a 401(k), or IRA, the taxes paid would be much less than the Proportional Rebalancing Strategy, for example, which would require_buying and selling of larger amounts of stocks and bonds every year. Of course, outside of a tax-sheltered account, the internal rebalancing of SSA would result in some taxable events but not near as onerous as selling larger amounts of stocks and bonds every year.

Of course, within a tax-sheltered account, there are no taxes paid on the balance until money is withdrawn, and this would hopefully happen only as planned for in retirement. If a Roth IRA is used, no taxes are paid after money is withdrawn either (those taxes are paid before the money is put in). I believe a Roth IRA is preferable to a traditional IRA, because the taxes are paid beforehand, and you never have to worry about them ever again. So, choose a Roth over traditional IRA if you can to cover the taxes at the beginning of your long-term savings plan.

In the sense that most stock is bought over time at lower prices, it may, at first, seem somewhat like the well-known Dollar Cost Averaging Strategy, but there is no basic similarity. That strategy (Dollar Cost Averaging) requires purchasing stock, usually on a regular schedule, through thick and thin, and in good markets and bad. The idea is that over time, more stock will be bought at lower prices as the market rises. The big problem with Dollar Cost Averaging is the regular purchase of substantial amounts of stock at overvalued prices. This is because the stock market can stay in an overvalued mode for a long time, forcing the Dollar Cost Averaging investor to buy a lot of this overvalued stock. That is rarely the case with SSA.

The stock market rises over time due primarily to corporate profits and inflation. This inflationary rise in the stock market will apparently "bail out" the Dollar Cost Averaging investor over time. That is what will seem to happen, at least on a non-inflation-adjusted or nominal basis. After the inflation factor is accounted for, an actual "bailout" is much less significant.

Why not buy primarily undervalued stocks, almost exclusively? Then, due to corporate profits, and on an inflation-adjusted basis (this will be documented in the next chapter), much higher real profits will be the result over time. Here is the strategy of this Strategic Stock Accumulation. All results in the back-testing process (Chapter 9) are in inflation-adjusted real numbers, as well as nominal numbers.

Probably the most common investment strategy today, practiced in one form or another, is Proportional Rebalancing. It includes the process of setting up an asset allocation and then rebalancing those assets back to their original percentages on a regular basis. This approach does force the investor to "buy low and sell higher," as will be documented within 6 different time periods over the last 84 years. It is frequently combined with some kind of a regular Dollar Cost Averaging component to add to the initial asset percentages over time. Unfortunately, this results in a mediocre way to accumulate assets. This will be shown, as a result of the back-testing process clearly laid out in Chapter 9.

Rebalancing, as explained earlier, does occur also within the Strategic Stock Accumulation Strategy. However, this rebalancing occurs **only between the individual stock and bond index funds** and does not rebalance the beginning stock/bond-cash ratio on an annual basis, as does Proportional Rebalancing. Rebalancing within SSA represents an added bonus effect but is not the primary driver of return, as it is in the PR Strategy.

Strategic Stock Accumulation (SSA) is, as will be shown through this back-testing process, consistently superior to Proportional Rebalancing and to a 100% All-Stock Strategy. **It is important to understand that the Strategic Stock Accumulation strategy explained in this chapter, is the same strategy I back-tested through six time periods.** I will compare the Proportional Rebalancing approach with Strategic Stock Accumulation Strategy. I will also compare these two strategies with a 100% 'buy and hold' All-Stock Strategy. All three of these strategies will be tested through six different time periods. The back-testing process used will be fully explained in the next chapter, "Back-Testing Three Strategies · through six different time periods.

A 100% All-Stock portfolio should only be attempted,

taking risk into consideration, for a younger or late middle-age investor. This strategy should not be used by anyone older than 55, in my opinion. The back-tested results confirmed this admonition. Severe stock market corrections have devastated All-Stock portfolios for several years or longer before the market regains momentum. An older investor or retiree may not have the time or inclination to wait for the market to "come back." It is true that a 56-year-old investor, for example, would probably have enough time to be "made whole" again before the necessity of spending down of invested assets in retirement begins. That is, if the investor doesn't sell any stock in a serious downturn and can handle a crash psychologically at this age. By psychologically, I mean the ability to sleep at night, without the worry of a decreased retirement living standard. This also assumes that the investor retires no earlier than 62 to 65.

However, investors in this age range start to face additional challenges, many of which are health-related. Older investors also tend to be more conservative and less psychologically adaptable to loss. Most do not wish to undergo the mental stress of worrying if their portfolio will regain its lost money as the result of a crash before they need it for daily retirement expenses.

The younger individual has the most valuable commodity, after basic investment knowledge, that an investor can possess—Time! The fact is, the more stock that he or she can accumulate during these younger decades, even if there are occasional overpayments, the better off the investor will be in his or her 60's and 70's. But youth also has its challenges, the biggest of which is maintaining discipline in the face of competing desires for current consumption. As a rule, young people want "things"! That's okay, except that it frequently interferes with the accumulation of sufficient assets for retirement. So, not controlling current consumption is a big financial mistake (at any age). This temptation can be overcome with discipline, perseverance, and a financial goal. And this temptation has to be overcome, if the younger (or middle-aged) investor wishes to retire financially independent.

Back-testing followed Strategic Stock Accumulation (SSA) and Proportional Rebalancing (PR), as well as a 100% All-Stock (AS) portfolio, through six severe stock market corrections (most of them considered crashes). The combination of 3 time periods together between 1972 and 2013 was also back-tested to show how all 3 strategies performed over a 41-year consecutive period. I will show the return results in the next chapter for each strategy. The earliest time period covered includes the so-called "Great Depression." The years I back-tested for this time period are 1928 year-end to 1939 year-end. The next time period is 1972–1988, also both year-end. This period included the Arab oil embargo and the hyperinflation of the late 70s. The third time period is 1999–2006, and includes the pricking of technology's "dot.com bubble," resulting after a long period of widespread investor "irrational exuberance." The next time period compared was 2006–2013.

The years 2007–2009 are considered by many people today to include the second greatest economic catastrophe in the U.S. after the "Great Depression" of the 1930s. This was the "Great Recession" of 2007–2009, and it is the one most remembered by people today. The last period back-tested is 1972–2013, and this was accomplished by adding three individual time periods: 1972–1988, 1988–1999, and 1999–2013. These 3 different time periods were added together to show how all 3 strategies performed (and compared) over a consecutive 41-year period.

Even though this is the subject of the next chapter, I have briefly summarized here what was back-tested and when. I want you to see that the Strategic Stock Accumulation Strategy you are about to learn in this chapter will be shown and documented to have a sound basis in the next chapter. While learning the strategy in this chapter, you can be confident the next chapter will show why this learning process, and its implementation, will be profitable.

At this point, let's start learning the SSA Strategy. Read the following "Steps" over at least three times. This is the most important part of the book! If you "Get" this, then you will be on your way to success as an investor for securing your financial future.

Strategic Stock Accumulation: The Steps

Steps 1 through 3 should be completed as soon as you decide to implement SSA, at any time of the year. Do not wait until calendar year-end to start the following three steps. The completion of these first three steps will result in the set up of your total asset allocation, including your particular Stock/Bond-Cash ratio. From that time on, wait until calendar year-end to determine if the 'Buy/Sell' rules apply in any given year. How to determine when, and if, any of the Buy/Sell Rules apply at calendar year-end is explained in Steps 4 through 6.

Step 1: CHOOSE THE INDEX FUNDS IN YOUR ASSET ALLOCATION (If Necessary, Review Chapter 6)

> Choose:
> Chart 1, 10 Stock Index Funds
> 2 Bond Funds
> 1 Money Market Fund
>
> Or:
> Chart 2, 8 Stock Index Funds
> 2 Bond Funds
> 1 Money Market Fund
> (As outlined in Chapter 6)

Step 2: DETERMINE A STOCK/BOND-CASH RATIO (If Necessary, Review Chapter 7)

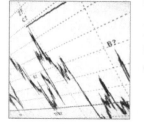

Determine which of the following stock/bond-cash ratios you will use based on your age, as outlined in Chapter 7:

> A - 65/35
> B - 50/50
> C - 35/65

Step 3: PLUG IN CHOSEN INDEX FUNDS TO YOUR STOCK/BOND-CASH RATIO

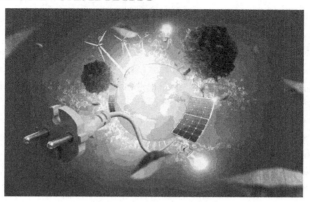

2 Examples:

Chart 1 Chosen Index Funds in Asset Allocation used with
      65/35 Stock/Bond-Cash Ratio
Chart 2 Chosen Index Funds in Asset Allocation used with
      35/65 Stock/Bond-Cash Ratio

Follow the SSA "Buy Rules" (rules for changing [i.e., buying]) original stock/bond-cash ratio during a stock market correction or crash (see Chart 3 below):

Step 4: MEMORIZE THE "BUY RULES" OF CHART 3

Follow the SSA "Buy Rules" (rules for changing [i.e., buying]) original stock/bond-cash ratio during a stock market correction or crash (see Chart 3 below):

CHART 3: "BUY RULES"

CHART 3: BUY RULES

1. Year-end stock market price (S&P 500) level must be at least 7% below previous year-end close.

2. Must follow Pyramid buying schedule, as shown in Chart 5, by buying increasingly higher dollar amounts (in percentage terms), as the stock market continues its descent. These stock purchases are made as these lower levels trigger buying, in 7% downward increments. The percentage buying is on a cumulative, or additive basis. For Example: if the market drops between 7% and 14% by year-end, then investor buys at 7% Pyramid Buy level (3.6%). If the next year-end close is down 9%, he would choose the 14% buy level as the appropriate buy percentage, which would be 10.7%. (See Pyramid Chart 5, Column 6). In this case the total amount of stock bought in percentage terms for both years would be 14.3% (3.6 plus 10.7).

3. As the stock market rises above the lowest point reached, on an annual basis, a new yearly low must be reached before any additional buying can occur. After three years, any 7% or greater decrease in the stock market, at year-end, is treated as a new correction or crash. In other words, buying according to the Pyramid Buy schedule resumes, regardless of any past stock market year-end closes of more than three years previous to current year-end close.

4. This Rule is similar to Rule 2, except that the emphasis is on the importance of not making stock purchases at year-end as on Column C, S&P 500 cumulative change column on all of the research tables. Purchases are made on a cumulative basis only from the crash years, as, for example on Column D of the tables at the end of the book. Only the present total years involved since the crash or correction started are cumulative for buying purposes. Buy levels are determined on a year-end to year-end basis, but all the years involved in the present crash are added up to determine what percentage Buy level the investor should use. For example, the S&P 500 may be down 35% on a cumulative basis, from it's highest level five years earlier, but only down 20% from the previous two years. Let's say the two year total of 20% down was comprised of 8% down the first year and 12% down the second year. Stock would be bought on the 20% number the second year, not the 12% or 35% figure. Of course, in this case the investor following SSA would have bought stock during the previous year-end, based on the 8% level at that time.

5. Rebalance within the individual stock and bond index funds on an annual basis (at year-end), if no rebalancing has occurred as a result of funds being sold according to the "Sell rules" (that process would have rebalanced "everything"). So the internal rebalancing does not mean rebalancing back to the original Stock/Bond-Cash Ratio. That process is determined by the "Sell" rules. It means rebalancing the stock index funds back to their individual equal percentage values, as show in Charts 1 and 2. The Bond-Cash rebalancing would occur also according to the investor's individual percentages from one of these charts.

Step 5: MEMORIZE THE "SELL RULES" OF CHART 4 Follow the SSA Sell Rules (Chart 4) for reestablishing (i.e., selling) beginning stock/bond cash ratio as a result of the stock market rising again up to its previous high.

CHART 4: "SELL RULES"

CHART 4: SELL RULES
1. Stock market (S&P 500) must have met its previous high since the most recent market crash.
2. P/E CAPE Index must be 20 or higher at year-end.
3. Federal Reserve must be raising interest rates at least 1% as shown by the 3-month T-Bill interest rate. It also must have risen at least one-half percent above the previous year-end close.
4. Inflation rate must have exceeded 2.75% annual average by year-end.
5. The "Buy Rules" always "trump" the "Sell Rules" . It is possible that both Buy and Sell rules could be triggered at year-end. In this case don't sell, but follow the "Buy Rules".
6. If the Federal Reserve raises interest rates past 2% at any point during the year, and all other Sell Rules are triggered, then Sell immediately. Do NOT wait until year-end! In all other cases, regarding Fed induced interest rates at or below 2%, this rule does not apply.

Step 6) MAINTAIN YOUR REESTABLISHED STOCK/BOND-CASH RATIO UNTIL NEXT STOCK MARKET CRASH OR CORRECTION (as determined at year-end and then rebalance between the funds at year-end).

Either of these situations (crash or correction) resulting in sufficient volatility to initiate action would dictate buying stock again according to the "Buy Rules" (see Chart 3). Until that point is reached, maintain the status quo (i.e., original ratio). However, you would still rebalance within the individual funds (but not the entire stock/bond-cash ratio) at year-end, as described earlier.

DESCRIBING THE STEPS IN DETAIL:

STEP 1: CHOOSING THE INDEX FUNDS IN YOUR AS-SET ALLOCATION

Review the process of choosing the index funds in your asset allocation as described in Chapter 6. The decision as to which asset allocation (Chart 1 or 2) to use in Strategic Stock Accumulation will have been made by this point. Both options, represented by Charts 1 and 2, provide more than adequate diversification, negative correlation, and therefore, risk reduction and rebalancing potential. All four of these investing concepts have been described in Chapter 6.

To review, diversification and correlation are related concepts that basically refer to the importance of "not putting all of your eggs into one basket." This diversification and negative correlation results in better portfolio risk reduction. However, there is an additional benefit resulting from adequate diversification and negative correlation within a portfolio: the additional return over time generated by the internal "rebalancing effect.'

Rebalancing, as described in Chapter 6, is the process of partially selling those assets that have appreciated to a greater degree than other assets in the portfolio. It also includes the process of buying more of those assets that have lagged or decreased in value over the period of one year (in the SSA Strategy). This internal stock and bond-cash rebalancing would be done in such a manner as to reestablish the initial asset allocation percentages (but not the overall stock/bond-cash ratio).

When the Sell rules have been triggered, on the other hand, the initial stock/bond-cash ratios would also be reestablished. However, in the absence of a sell or buy trigger, the only changes resulting from rebalancing at year-end would be to reestablish the equal stock percentages, as indicated by the percentage each index fund represents in the portfolio chosen from either Asset Allocation Chart 1 or 2. The amount of individual bond-cash index fund percentages reestablished would also be those indicated by either chosen Asset Allocation Chart (1 or 2).

The only difference between Asset Allocation Chart 1 and Chart 2 is the addition of two extra funds in the stock portion of Chart 1. Those funds are the Precious Metals Fund and the Real Estate Investment Trust Fund. Chart 1 includes 10 stock funds, while Chart 2 has 8 funds. Some investors may not wish to include precious metals or real estate in their portfolio. They would choose the Chart 2 Asset Allocation option to invest with the SSA Strategy. Once the asset allocation decision has been made, the next step is to choose a stock/bond-cash ratio.

STEP 2: DETERMINE A STOCK/BOND-CASH RATIO

Let's now determine your stock/bond-cash ratio (also see Chapter 7). This ratio will be selected from three options: 65/35, 50/50, or 35/65. The reason for these three ratios is that we want to have a balance between having at least enough in stock in the market at all times to take advantage of the stock market in a "bull" mode, but even more importantly, enough bond-cash "ammunition" to take advantage of corrections and crashes. In the next chapter on back-testing, the three ratios listed above will be referred to repeatedly.

Let's describe these ratios again in a little more detail. A 50/50 stock/bonds-cash ratio means that within an investor's portfolio, there exists 50% stock (in the form of different stock index funds making up the stock portion of the investor's asset allocation), and bonds and cash comprise the other 50%. This bonds-cash portion would be further broken down between bonds and cash, based on the asset allocation as reflected in Chart 1 or 2, as the investor had previously decided upon.

As stated earlier, the breakdown of bonds and cash within both asset allocation choices, percentage-wise, and in terms of duration, is done in such a way as to allow a fast conversion to stock when the time requires. The stock/bond-cash ratio decision should be made based on an investor's age, as explained in Chapter 6, "Choosing the Index Funds for Your Asset Allocation." For example, a 24-year-old investor, just getting started in the stock market, would appropriately choose the 65/35 stock/bond-cash beginning ratio. On the other hand, a 65-year-old retiree is better off starting with a 35/65 ratio.

Don't worry about the profit potential of the more heavily weighted bond-cash portfolio (and lower stock-weighted). As I'll show you in the next chapter, the 50/50 ratio actually had the second highest return of all 3 ratios, and all 3 strategies back-tested over a 41-year period (see Chart 9). The reason for this is the high amount of cash available to buy stock "on sale" during corrections and crashes. If you are younger and using the more highly weighted stock ratio of 65/35, then you should know that this stock/bond-cash ratio did best over the 41-year period tested (1972–2013, Chart 9) of all ratios and all 3 strategies! Going forward, it is best for this age group to have most of its investment in the stock market, of all three ratios, at all times.

STEP 3: PLUG INDEX FUNDS INTO YOUR STOCK/BOND-CASH RATIO:

Once you have chosen the index funds in your asset allocation and determined your stock/bonds-cash ratio, it is a simple matter to plug these index funds into your into your stock/bonds-cash ratio. The result of this combination will represent your particular total asset allocation. It will also be the beginning of your particular SSA Strategy in the stock and bond markets. Now you are ready to learn the implementation of Strategic Stock Accumulation. Keep in mind that your stock/bonds-cash ratio will change as stock is bought (Buy Rules Chart 3) during market corrections and crashes. As stock is purchased, obviously, this stock portion of the ratio will increase. And then, as the Sell Rules of Chart 4 are triggered, the original stock/bonds-cash ratio will be reestablished.

STEP 4: FOLLOWING THE "BUY RULES"

"Follow the SSA "Buy Rules" of Chart 3. These rules show how to buy additional stock in the form of index funds during a market crash or correction at year-end. This action, of course, will change the investor's stock/bond-cash ratio, which will not be reestablished until the Sell Rules trigger just the right amount of stock sale for this to happen. The Buy Rules are as follows:

1) Year-end S&P 500 stock index price level must be at

least 7% below the previous year-end close.

2) Follow the Pyramid buying schedule, as shown in Chart 5, by buying with increasingly higher dollar amounts (in percentage terms), as the stock market continues its descent. These purchases are made at year-end, as these lower levels in 7% downward increments are triggered. The purchase percentages are <u>additive.</u> In other words, for example, if the stock market is down 42% during the second year-end of a market crash, and was down 9% the previous year-end, then, at second year-end use 100% of the remaining bond-cash position (see Pyramid Chart 5, Column 5) of the portfolio to buy additional stock (9% plus 42% equals 51%). This 100% stock purchase with the remaining funds in the bond-cash portion would occur even though 3.6% (bought at the 7% trigger level) of a larger bond-cash position was used to buy stock the previous year-end.

3) If the stock market rises above the lowest point reached and then starts to descend again, then a new low must be reached before any additional stock buying can occur, unless three years have gone by without a new market low being reached. At that point, any 7% or more decrease in the stock market is treated as a new correction or crash. The next year-end purchase, if any, would be made at the 14% level or more, below the new crash or correction level. Why at least 14%? Because the previous year's 7% level must be added to any purchase in the following year. These figures would be calculated at year-end, and any appropriate buy action is taken at that time.

4) The buy levels are determined on a cumulative basis for the years involved in the present crash only. For example, the S&P 500 may be down 35% on a cumulative basis from 6 years earlier, before the present market crash began, but only 20% down from the year before. We would buy based on the 20% number, reflecting the present crash, not the 35%. It also may be the case that the SSA investor had bought stock during the previous years, based on those individual year-end numbers. Also keep in mind that YOU ARE ONLY BUYING, AT MOST, ONCE PER YEAR AT YEAR-END!

5) Rebalance within the individual stock and bond index funds once per year. As individual stock and bond funds outperform one another on an annual basis, sell enough dollar amounts of those outperforming funds and buy enough additional amounts of the lagging funds to rebalance (i.e., reestablish) back to the original equal percentages in the stock portion of your asset allocation. Also rebalance to the appropriate percentages in the bond-cash portion of your portfolio. This would not, however, reestablish your beginning stock/bond-cash ratio (which would actually occur only if all the Sell Rules were triggered), but only rebalance the individual percentages as indicated in your asset allocation.

Following the Buy Rules correctly is the most important part of buying increasing amounts of stock index funds (at year-end), as the stock market decline continues during a correction or crash. This has been made easy, by following the Pyramid Buy Levels of Chart 5. The ease of this process psychologically could be a challenge for some investors in the beginning. Some may find it difficult at first to buy as the stock market retreats, since it may be hard initially for them to do something that may seem counter-intuitive.

CHART 5 – PYRAMID BUY LEVELS

1	2	3	4	5	6
% Decline Trigger	Algebraic Multiplier		Cumulative Xs	Divided by Total # of Xs (28)	% of Remaining Total of Bond-Cash Used to Buy Stock
7%	x		x	1 ÷ 28 =	3.6%
14%	2x	+ x =	3x	3 ÷ 28 =	10.7%
21%	3x	+ 3x =	6x	6 ÷ 28 =	21.4%
28%	4x	+ 6x =	10x	10 ÷ 28 =	35.7%
35%	5x	+ 10x =	15x	15 ÷ 28 =	53.6%
42%	6x	+ 15x =	21x	21 ÷ 28 =	75.0%
49%	7x	+ 21x =	28x	28 ÷ 28 =	100.0%
TOTAL	28x				

CHART 5: Pyramid Buy Levels (Columns 1 and 6)

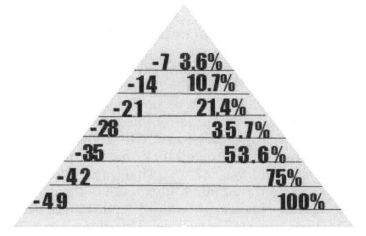

To buy while an investor thinks that money is continuing to be lost (on paper only) in the stock market may seem crazy. This may be considered a radical concept, in spite of the fact that most will realize, on many levels, that it is the right thing to do. Most humans are capable of adapting to new information, if they are able to understand that it can increase their chances of survival; in this case we are talking about the chance for financial survival (as well as the opportunity to thrive financially).

If someone truly realizes the wisdom of buying when others are selling, and selling when others are buying, he or she can succeed very well in the stock market, especially by following the SSA Strategy. Remember Warren Buffett's philosophy has always been to buy when others are selling, and sell when others are buying.

It is very important to: #1) understand the Strategic Stock Accumulation system, and how it is implemented. And #2) realize and be willing to accept that by virtue of the fact you are buying stock as the market declines, possibly up to 50% or more, it is a certainty that your portfolio will initially reflect much of that stock market decline, and probably show large losses on paper. The

**entire strategy of SSA is based on an initial port-
folio loss to result in a later large portfolio gain as
the stock market retraces back to its previous high
and beyond. This retracement, however, may not
occur for several years or more, although the
average bear market has lasted about 18 months.**

The primary idea behind the Pyramid Chart 5 is to focus
on a system that dictates exactly how to <u>buy ever increasing</u>
amounts of stock, in dollar as well as percentage terms, as
the stock market continues to retreat. Looking at Chart 6,
we can see that the average stock market decline over 6
time periods tested was 48.7%. That's the average. If we
can follow a system that takes advantage of these inevitable
corrections and crashes, we would have found the "Holy
Grail" of "bear market" investing. This describes the basis
of the Pyramid Buying Strategy.

How did I determine the 'buy levels' of the Pyramid
Chart? I first estimated a worst-case stock market crash
scenario of 50% down. This was very close to the average
stock market crash figure of 48.7% as mentioned above. I
then divided the 50% drop into 7 different groups: 7%,
14%, 21%, 28%, 35%, 42%, and 49% (close enough to 50%).
Then, I used a simple algebraic equation for matching percentage drops in the stock market with exact dollar
percentages of purchase. For example, I gave a value of "X"
for a 7% down (X=7%), 2x for 14% down, 3x for 21% down,
etc., up to 7x for 49% down. Adding up all the Xs, we get
28, or 28x = 100%. Now, at a drop in the stock market of
16%, I would buy at a level thrice (3x) the level of an 8% (X)
drop in the market. Likewise, at a 49% drop in the market,
I would be buying at a 7x level (much higher, at 100%). Any
drop seen between two percentages is calculated to the
lower percentage for buying purposes. In other words, a
26% market drop is matched with the 21% level (3x), not
with the 28% (4x) level.

<u>Our goal is to use up most, if not all, of our bond-cash
portion of the portfolio by buying stock "on sale" in any
crash reaching the 49%-or-greater level on a cumulative
basis.</u>

So, as the stock market drops, more stock is bought at

higher percentages. However, this does not represent an exact linear relationship between the Xs. In other words, the SSA investor does not buy exactly twice the amount of stock at 14% (2x) down as at 7% (X). The increased percentage bought at each progressive drop of 7%, was determined by dividing the total number of Xs (28) into the number of Xs represented by the particular percentage drop in the stock market. In other words, if the stock market drops 22% by year-end, we would buy at the 3x level (21%), right? So, we would divide the total number of Xs up into 3x (x plus 2x plus 3x equals 6x—Chart 5, Column 4), by the total number of all Xs up to 7x (28). So, 6 divided by 28 is 21.4% (Chart 5, Columns 5 and 6).

Now, it's very important to understand that if the crash or correction causes the market to retreat further the following year, then the 22% previous year-end multiplier would be added to whatever percent multiplier is determined for the present year-end. As should be fairly obvious, we want to buy a lot of stock during a market crash!

You now know how much of our bond-cash position at year-end should be used to buy additional stock: 21.4%. The same process is used to determine buying levels at all other percentage drops in the market between 7% and 49% (or greater). Any cumulative drop from the start of the crash or correction above 49% is treated as if it was a 49% drop by that particular year-end. In other words, 100% of the remaining bond-cash position would be used to buy additional stock at that point.

Again, these purchases would all take the form of exchange-traded index funds with the type determined by the investor's asset allocation. Review Charts 1 through 5 until they are thoroughly understood. All stock index fund purchases during this process would be bought in such a way as to equalize all the dollar amounts in the stock portion of the portfolio. In following this method, you would allocate more money to buy some funds and less money to buy others, depending upon which funds had increased or decreased in value up to that point. The total amount of dollars spent would depend on the Pyramid Chart 5. This would not, however, reestablish your particular stock/bond-cash ratio.

As you can see, after buying stock during a market crash or correction, the stock portion of your ratio would increase. The only time your stock/bond-cash ratio would be exactly reestablished would be when a portfolio sale is triggered by all six Sell Rules being activated. At that point, enough stock would be sold to result in the investor's exact individual stock/bond-cash ratio. This will be explained further in the next step: Following the Sell Rules.

The Pyramid Strategy of buying increasing amounts of stock, in higher percentages and as the stock market continues to decline further into apparent "portfolio loss" territory, is what increases the profit potential of SSA significantly over a 100% "buy and hold" stock strategy, for example (and also over a Proportional Rebalancing Strategy, which will be documented in the next chapter on back-testing).

Chart 3 shows the "Buy Rules" of SSA. Within the stock portion, you already know which index funds to include and in what percentages. I've discussed the importance of using index funds (in the form of ETFs), as opposed to individual stocks and "managed" funds. We will purchase index funds at year-end, based on triggering of these Buy Rules. Again, the Pyramid Buy Levels of Chart 5 show the actual mechanics of how this is done. This is the true 'center,' or baseline, of the SSA Strategy.

We will use the Pyramid Buy purchase approach, as shown in Chart 5. What this means is that as the market continues to drop, greater amounts (in percentages) of stock will be bought in the form of a pyramid, which gets larger and larger as the bottom is reached. Why do we buy even greater dollar amounts (higher percentages) of stock as the market continues to decline? Isn't this even more risky? I hope you can see by now that following this strategy is what is ultimately so profitable. For example, when the stock market is down between 7%, but not yet 14%, the investor uses only 3.6% of his bond/cash total to buy additional stock (Chart 5, Column 1 and 6).

On the other hand, when the stock market is down

between 42% and 49%, he or she would use 75% of the remaining amount in the bond/cash portion of the portfolio to buy more stock (Chart 5, Column 1 and 6).The percentages used to buy any level of additional stock are all shown in Chart 5, Column 6. It doesn't matter which stock/bond-cash ratio the investor uses, the percentage of the remaining bond/cash amount used to buy additional stock would be the same, all based on Columns 1 and 6 of Pyramid Chart 5. Of course, as explained earlier, any previous year-end percentage buying would be added to the present year-end percentage buying to give an overall total percentage of stock bought at the present year-end. Crash year buying is additive.

These dollar amounts and percentages, of course, refer to the bond-cash portion of the ratio, since this represents the part of the portfolio that will be used to purchase additional stock, after it is converted to cash.

It's important to also remember that after money has left the bond/cash portion of the portfolio, to buy additional stock, that the remaining money in the bond-cash portion is readjusted to reflect the actual percentages in the investor's asset allocation. This will probably involve some additional buying and selling within that portion of the portfolio. If this sounds complicated, you may rest in knowing that it really isn't after you've done it once. Also, any buying using the Pyramid Buy chart happens only once per year, at most. Buying, based on this chart, may not occur for another five years or more! This depends totally on how the Buy Rules are triggered. There is also no reason to be concerned if the Buy (or Sell) Rules are not triggered. There could many years when this is the case, and it's important to do nothing during these times!

We will assume, as another example, we are starting with a $100,000 total portfolio. Initial bond-cash balances could be $50,000 for a 50/50 stock/bonds-cash ratio, $65,000 for a 35/65 stock/bonds-cash ratio, and $35,000 for a 65/35 stock/bonds-cash ratio. We will buy additional stock as outlined in Chart 3 and Chart 5 (Column 6) at 7% downward intervals in the stock market. So, from year to year, on an additive basis, we buy at 7% down, then 14%

down, 21%, 28%, 35%, 42%, and finally at 49% down.

Why stop at 49%? Because a worst-case scenario of about a 50% drop in the stock mark was chosen. As mentioned earlier, the average drop in the market during the typical crash is 48.7%. Of course, the stock market could drop further, as it sometimes has in the past, but, if it does fall below 50%, we would still have bought a lot of stock at very cheap prices and will profit extremely well, as the market retraces to its previous high, and then beyond.

Remember, the stock market always comes back, eventually. Sometimes it does take longer. Older and/or retired investors do need to keep in mind what John Maynard Keynes, the 19th century British economist said about us all being "dead in the long run" (meaning even though the stock market always comes back in the long run, we may be dead before it does)." This is the reason for the 35/65 stock/bond-cash ratio recommendation for investors over 55 years of age. At the same time, the Federal Reserve's ability, and its inclination to provide almost instant liquidity during a market crash or severe correction, means that we are talking about an average of about 18 months per bear market over the last 80 years.

Let's use another example of how we would use Chart 5 to buy stock. Chart 5 (the Pyramid Buying Strategy) is set up to be able to use increasing amounts of our bonds-cash to purchase stock as the market drops during a correction or crash. Again, we use the simple algebraic equation to determine the increasing percentages. For example, as shown in Columns 1 and 2, we would use "X" amount of dollars at 7% down (X = 7%), 2"x" at 14% down, 3"x" at 21% down, and so forth, until we spent 7"x" at 49% down (7x = 49%). Then to solve for "X," we divide the relevant number of "X"s (at the present year-end) in Column 4 by 28 (This is the total number of Xs). This gives us 3.6% for "X" and a dollar value of X of $1,800 ($50,000 times 3.6%, as shown in Column 6). We would then multiply $50,000 by 3.6%, yielding $1,800. So, at 7% down in the stock market, we would buy an additional $1,800 worth of stock.

If the stock market drops between 14% and 21% at the next year-end, this time the investor would buy an additional $10,315 worth of stock index funds (Column 6). Why $10,315? Because this represents 21.4% (Chart 5, Columns 1 and 6.) of $48,200 ($50,000 minus $1,800). A 7% decline trigger (first year-end) plus 14% decline trigger (second year-end) equals 21% (remember, these figures are additive) decline trigger. (We multiply the remaining bond-cash total at that year-end point times 21.4% (column 6), which corresponds to the 21% trigger (column 1). We must first, however, subtract $1,800 from the original $50,000 to leave $48,200. We then multiply the $48,200 times 21.4% to get $10,315. As you can see, if the market drops to at least 49% down over one or more years in a row, we would use 100% of our <u>remaining</u> bond-cash portion of the portfolio, whatever that amount is by that year-end time.

As per your individual Asset Allocation Chart, you will have the bond-cash total, in a short-term U.S. bond fund, a short-term U.S. Treasury inflation protected securities (TIPS) bond fund, and the rest in a liquid U.S. money market fund. Interest rates are due to rise, and they probably will at some point in 2015. As of the writing of this book, it is now July, 2014. There are two reasons for using index bond funds and also for the short-term duration of this bond-cash portion of the portfolio: One, short-term U.S. index bond funds can be sold quickly with much less risk of a large capital loss, as may even occur with longer duration U.S. bond funds, and two: Any individual bond, as opposed to any index bond fund, will probably not have the same liquidity as the index bond fund does. In other words, it may take longer to sell at a fair market price.

Bonds are now close to "bubble" territory. This is because there has been a 32-year bull market in bonds, as long-term interest rates have continued to decrease over the entire 30-year period. In other words, when interest rates go down, bond values go up, and vice-versa; when interest rates are rising, bond values go down!

This, at first, sounds counter-intuitive. After all, if interest rates go up, that means bonds pay a higher interest rate, right? And if they go down, that must mean they pay a lower interest rate, and that should be bad for bonds. This is all very true for newly issued bonds, but not for already existing bonds. The trick is to think of the bond market as consisting of those bonds that investors, or the public, already own. So, if I own a ten-year U.S. government bond paying 5% annually, and interest rates rise one percentage point to 6%, this means all other 10 year government bonds, which I do not own, now adjust to pay 6% and my 5% bond is worth one percentage point less in the bond market, if I want to sell it. One percentage point or, as it is termed in the bond market, 100 basis points, may not sound like much, but since it represents a 20% (5 by divided by 1) increase in interest rates, it could lead to a 15 to 25% capital loss in the value of the bond! I would then have to sell the bond for less (a discount), so that the lower discounted selling price would allow a buyer of the bond to get an effective 6% return on my bond, because he is paying less for it. For example, a $1000 US bond at 5% would yield $50/year.

If interest rates rise to 6%, then the new 10 year bonds are now yielding $60/year, and I, as a seller, must be happy with a selling price of $833.33, which is reached by dividing the old interest rate of 5% by the new interest rate of 6% and multiplying that quotient, .8333, by the $1000 value of the bond when it was first issued at 5%.

You can now see how higher interest rates are bad for all existing bonds, and lower interest rates are good for those bonds. In the case of lower interest rates, let's say they moved from 5% to 4%. Then, as a seller, I will be happy with a selling price of $1250 for a $250 profit. This is reached by dividing the old 5% interest rate by the new 4% interest rate, and then multiplying this quotient by the $1000 initial value of the bond. I make a profit because the buyer must pay me a premium of $250 in order to equal the old 5% interest on the bond. If he buys a newly issued bond at 4%, it would only pay $1000, but then he must be satisfied with only a 4% return. It doesn't matter which option he takes, buying my bond or a newly issued one, he still is only going to get a net return of 4%.

Presently, the ten-year bond starting back from 2009 is yielding under 2.5%, a rate not seen in over 30 years. Money market funds are yielding less than one-fourth of

1%. These rates are much less than the present inflation rate of just over 2% per year. This means that anyone who has money in cash is losing almost 2% a year to inflation. However, investors stand to lose a lot more by investing in longer-duration bonds. Rebalancing within the bond-cash portion of the portfolio will also act as a counterweight to rising interest rates and should provide additional return over time.

When interest rates start rising again, many long-term bond investors will have a rude awakening, especially if they never rebalance. Many of these people have been scared away from the stock market, because they suffered severe losses in the past. Many of them sold their stock holdings at or near the stock market bottom in 2002 and 2009. Now, they will lose more money in the bond market, as interest rates inevitably rise. <u>As you can see, it is very dangerous to be financially illiterate.</u> Everyone needs to have a basic understanding of markets or eventually suffer the consequences, if they invest at all, in stocks or bonds. In the long run, short-term bonds are important to the SSA portfolio. And we are concerned, primarily, with the long run.

In spite of the precarious situation in the bond market today, many financial advisers still recommend that investors keep a significant percentage of their portfolio in long-term bonds. I'm convinced most of them do this only because they always have, and since many are doing it, they can claim it is "normal" and "prudent" advice. Baloney! Most investors should stay short term, especially at this point in time, regardless of what strategy is followed. And be skeptical concerning what most of the "experts" are saying at any point in time. I am no exception (and I'm not calling myself an expert). Use your own judgment as to the merits of Strategic Stock Accumulation. Study the back-testing results. Does this strategy make sense to you? If, after spending some time in evaluating it, you cannot see its merits, then it is not for you. I believe, however, that if you just learn the basics of investing by reading and studying this book (and this chapter two to three times), then you will have a good foundation on the way to controlling your own financial destiny.

Let's review once more how we would determine how much additional stock to buy from Chart 5 during a stock market crash or correction. We simply find the percent decline trigger figure that applies (Column 1). We then look for the corresponding percentage in Column 6. This percentage would be added to any previous crash year buying percentages. This total percentage would then be multiplied by the remaining balance in the bond-cash portion of the portfolio to determine how much total stock to buy that year-end.

For example, let's say the bond-cash portion of an overall 50/50 stock/bonds-cash portfolio is $175,000. Let's further assume that the stock market has dropped 38%. This figure is above 35% and below 42% (column 1). So, we would look at Column 6 in the Pyramid Buy Levels chart to see what percentage corresponds to 35% (Column 1)—and that is 53.6%. The investor would then multiply $175,000 times 53.6%. This would yield $93,800. If this was the first year of the crash, then we would use this amount of our bonds-cash position to purchase more stock. The types and amounts of stock index funds we buy will correspond to the types and percentages in our personal asset allocation.

Please reread the previous paragraph several times and become very familiar with the Buy and Sell Rules in Charts 3 and 4, as well as the Pyramid Buy Levels of Chart 5. It will be well worth understanding these three charts in order to successfully implement the strategy of SSA. Once you've got it, it will be easy to use after that. Once you use the strategy during a market correction, or crash, you will forever see stock market crashes, or corrections (of 7% or more), in a different light.

CHART 6: S&P 500— Six Stock Market Crashes

The average investor thinks of a stock market crash as some sort of abnormal economic occurrence, something that should not have happened, or something that's very wrong. Therefore, it must be someone's fault. This "someone" is usually the bankers, speculators, or even the Federal Reserve printing too much money. You need to get this out of your head. I repeat "get this out of your head." That kind of negative thinking can never help an investor.

CHART 6: STOCK MARKET CRASHES

SIX S&P 500 STOCK MARKET CRASHES			
Crash Years	% Total Consecutive Year Losses	% Amount Of Stock Bought From Bond/Cash	% Pyramid Level of Purchase Reached
1929-1932	-101.9%	100%	49%
1937	-35.7%	53.6%	35%
1973-1974	-43.3	75%	42%
2000-2002	-42.4%	75%	42%
2007-2008	-40.36%	53.6%	35%
1938-1941	-28.6%	35.7%	28%
Total 84 years Covered	Average: 48.7%	Average: 65.5%	Average: 38.5%
21 Years of Market Crashes or 25% of Time			

The fact of the matter is, for every "boom," there will be a "bust," pure and simple—always has been and always will be. No one can predict exactly when the bust will occur, but as the night follows the day, it will recur, at regular intervals over an investor's lifetime. Remember, 25% of the time, historically, we are in a "bear market" (when stock market goes down). I guess that means one out of every four years, on average, we have to go through this "blame game" exercise.

By the way, those bankers and speculators, and even the "printing press Fed," all had a big part to play in also bringing on the "boom" years. The Fed provided plenty of liquidity in the form of low interest rates and printed dollars. The banks spread this easy money around, with low or no money down mortgages and other low interest loans. And the speculators helped drive prices up through the stratosphere by continuing to buy, many times on large amounts of credit. They were the ones responsible for all of those 401(k)s gaining more than14% a year for over a decade prior to the "dot-com bubble" crash of 2000.

The "Fed" and the "greedy bankers" were responsible, in large part, for housing prices going up in value almost every year prior to 2007, by a lot! Nobody said: "Please stop my stock portfolio from going up so fast; there must be something wrong, I don't think I deserve all of this easy money I'm making in the stock market," or "someone has to stop my house from going up so much in value every year; it just doesn't seem fair." Everyone was happy, just going along for the ride, until the gravy train stopped. Then it was blame game time.

We didn't earn those out-sized ridiculous returns, especially in the 90s. But we thought that we did, and that the money was ours to spend and borrow against, just the same. So, people get upset when the market takes it all away through a stock market crash. And then we hear: "The stock market is rigged. I'll never go into it again.

"Well, don't despair! You can beat the market by buying stock and then rebalancing when it goes too far the other way (even if it is rigged, which it isn't, especially for a long-term investor) as it becomes increasingly undervalued. Buy then and make big profits later, as the stock market retraces back up to its previous high and beyond. You can do this by following the strategy of SSA laid out in this book.

Keep in mind, you won't have "earned" these profits either, but they will be yours, just the same. That is the stock market in our capitalist economy. Don't fight it, rail against it, or try to make it fit your worldview. Just accept it as is and learn how to profit from it. So, get the SSA Strategy mentally internalized, and "welcome' the next stock market crash.

For purposes of comparing apples with apples during the back-testing process, I showed what would have happened if an investor waited until the end of the year before purchasing additional stock as per the pyramid buying procedure outlined on Chart 5. There are several reasons for buying only once per year; one is simplicity. The once-a-year decision-making allows the investor to make any stock purchases according to the Buy Rules under relatively stress-free conditions. He or she can study the Buy Rules at leisure to see how they may apply during the final months of the year.

The other important reason is that if the investor waits until year-end to buy, as back-testing bears out, many times he can buy greater amounts of stock at even lower prices, especially during a longer, secular bear market of two years or more. In other words, during this type of longer bear market, if he buys during the beginning of a market correction when the market is only down 8%, let's say, he would start his stock buying at a higher price than if he waits until year-end when the market is likely to be down even further.

Waiting until year-end to buy, if the Buy Rules are triggered, should allow more stock to be bought "on sale" at lower prices during a bear market lasting several years. He is "keeping his powder dry" for a longer period of time before using up most of his cash and bonds buying stock at possibly higher prices. However, the other side of the coin is that he may miss the chance to buy during occasional minor stock market corrections that right themselves before the end of the year. I believe year-end buying is most profitable over the long run, all things considered.

One important caveat: it's important to have at least 3–6 months' worth of emergency funds, independent of your dollars invested in SSA. I can't emphasize this strongly enough. You don't want to be in a position where you are forced to sell stock at or near the bottom of the market in order to cover an emergency or just routine living expenses. This is even more important for retirees. At least 8–10 years' worth of living expenses should be provided for (include Social Security in this calculation) outside the SSA Strategy. TIPS, or Treasury inflation-protected securities, are an excellent way to get this covered. If an investor had $10,000 in TIPS in a portfolio in the year 2000, for example, its purchasing power, even if it had a 0% interest yield for 14 years, would still have the purchasing power of the full $10,000 that it had in year 2000—14 years later! The principal of these bonds are adjusted semi-annually, to reflect changes in inflation, based on the CPI (consumer price index). This is important, especially for retirees, who are always concerned about inflation eating away their savings.

STEP 5: FOLLOWING THE "SELL RULES"

"Follow the SSA Sell Rules (Chart 4) for reestablishing (selling) the investor's individual stock/bond-cash ratio, as a result of those six rules triggering such a sale. This usually means the stock market has risen past its previous high.

1) Stock market must have at least met its previous high reached since before the most recent market crash, at year-end.

2) The P/E-10 ratio (CAPE index) MUST BE 20 or higher at year-end.

3) The Federal Reserve must be raising interest rates, as shown by a rising 3-month U.S. T-bill interest rate above 1%. I use the 3-month U.S. Treasury Bill because that was the benchmark interest source used in the back-testing. It's easy to find, and it closely correlates with the Federal Funds rate. If the Fed "sits tight" (does not raise interest rates), and this results in a 3-month Treasury Bill rate of 1% or less, do not sell until this Fed policy changes. If the Federal Funds rate is under 1%, and the Fed starts to raise interest rates, wait until the 3-month T-bill goes over 1% before considering this a "Sell" indicator.

If the Fed is raising the federal funds rate, and this results in a 3-month T-bill interest rate above 2%, and the other 5 Sell Rules are also triggered, then do not wait until year-end—sell immediately! (Rule 6). This is the only exception to the other five year-end only Buy/Sell Rules.

There is a very old but true Wall Street maxim that states: "don't fight the Fed." Fed-caused higher interest rates are, in general, eventually poison to the stock market. This usually causes a market drop within weeks or months. But, why wait? It's very important that this Sell timing exception be understood. It is well worth learning and following.

Again, the federal funds rate is the interest that banks must pay when borrowing overnight from another bank or from the Federal Reserve itself. This is the first way the Fed tries to control inflation and overall employment. You are probably wondering, "How do I know when the Fed is raising interest rates?" And, "Where do I find this information?" The simplest and quickest way is to <u>search on Google for this question, "Is the Federal Reserve raising interest rates at this time?"</u> And even more importantly, search on Google for <u>"What is the three-month T-bill interest rate at this time?"</u> Many different internet sites will pop up with this information. Usually the first one or two sites are the quickest way to get this information.

4) The Inflation rate must have reached an average of 2.75% or more for the year, by year-end. This would indicate that Fed action to increase interest rates has begun or is imminent. 2.75% is a somewhat arbitrary number, but Federal Reserve Board members get nervous as the inflation rate exceeds 2 to 2.25%. Fed action as a result of inflation exceeding this number is tempered by the employment situation. If the Fed thinks that the unemployment rate is too high, they believe this indicates greater "slack" in the economy. This slack will tend to keep a lid on rising prices, at least for a while. That is because if fewer people are working, fewer people are spending. This will tend to moderate any price increases. In that situation, the Fed is more likely to wait before starting to tighten (raise interest rates). The 2.75% inflation figure (assuming it goes up to that point) is a good indication that the employment situation is getting better, and that the Fed will begin raising

interest rates soon.

You can watch the unemployment rate to get a feel for coming inflation. This increases your ability to stay ahead of the curve. The internet is also great for finding this kind of information. Simply <u>search on Google for "What is the present unemployment rate?"</u> and "I<u>s the unemployment rate rising?"</u> Also search on Google for <u>"What is the present inflation rate,"</u> and "I<u>s the inflation rate rising?"</u> Again, you probably only need to stay on top of this once per year. You are almost always selling, at most, once per year, the only exception being Sell Rule 6. How simple is that? Also, you never buy, according to the Buy Rules, except at year-end. The exception to the above two statements is the annual year-end internal rebalancing. But, this takes place outside of the 'sell' rules, as explained earlier.

5) If both the Buy and Sell Rules are triggered at the same time by year-end, then buy, don't sell! The Buy Rules trump the Sell Rules.

6) If the Fed raises the federal funds rate to the extent the 3-month T-Bill interest rates raises past 2%, and all other Sell Rules indicate sell, then sell. Sell regardless of the time of year. But, all six Sell Rules must be triggered to sell any stock before year-end. Remember, don't fight the Fed! If the stock market has been in bull mode for a considerable period of time, the SSA investor will have reaped the profits accordingly by buying large amounts of stock "on sale." He should then stay increasingly aware of the greater likelihood of Fed action to start raising interest rates in order to "cool things off." This would be the only exception to the timing of all the other Sell Rules. However, all six Sell Rules must be triggered to sell <u>during</u> the year. If you are not seeing any possible near-term Federal Reserve interest rate changes in the course of the regular daily media news, then I would start checking on these figures at the beginning of December.

Let's look a little closer at these Sell Rules. Sell Rule 1 states, "The stock market must have met its previous high since the most recent crash." If this indicates a partial stock index fund sale should occur, then we look to the other the other five rules of the Sell strategy. Again, all six rules must indicate "sell" before we take that action. The P/E-10 ratio must be 20 or higher. The P/E-10 CAPE ratio is a very good indication of overall stock market valuation. This ratio was devised by Graham and Dodd over 60 years ago and more currently repopularized by Robert Shiller (Nobel Laureate in economics).

The P/E-10 RATIO shows the average price/earnings ratio, over the last 10 years on an inflation-adjusted basis. This gives a more accurate valuation of the market than only looking back one year, as it is commonly calculated. The P/E-10 is also better than a one-year forward estimate of this ratio. If the P/E-10 ratio is 20 or higher, then the stock market is probably overvalued, or at least moving strongly in that direction. It may even be overvalued at 17 or higher, so the 20 figure may be a little high and is somewhat arbitrary. It is not meant to indicate the exact start of market overvaluation.

The P/E- 10 RATIO has been added to the Sell Rules to help put a check on an investor's possible "irrational exuberance" (also Shiller's term). The stock market could be overvalued under conditions in which we would not sell stock to reestablish our original stock/bond-cash ratio. Those conditions would include any of the other five rules not being triggered. In other words, *all* six Sell Rules must apply before the SSA investor would sell any stock.

Sell Rule 3 states that: "Federal Reserve must be raising interest rates as evidenced by a rising 3-month Treasury Bill (T-bill) interest rate above 1%. It also must have risen at least 1/2% above previous year-end close." The 3-month T-bill will closely approximate the federal funds rate, so don't worry about much of a difference. If the Fed's last action was to lower interest rates, then we would never sell until at least this easier Fed policy changes. The most direct way the Fed starts its tightening process is by raising the interest rate banks must pay to borrow money from other banks and from the Federal Reserve itself. Banks will borrow money to maintain their reserve requirements. This is the Fed's required ratio of money on hand to money lent out.

The Fed engages in what is called "financial repression"

when it wishes to pay off more of the nation's debt from extremely high levels, relative to average historical levels. This is happening right now in July, 2014, just as it did after World War II. That war resulted in a very large debt overhang, causing the Fed to keep interest rates very low during the late 1940s and 1950s. It pays down this debt by keeping short-term rates near 0% for extended periods of time. This will eventually stimulate the economy and also reduce the chances of another recession, until rates start to rise again. The Fed hopes medium- and long-term interest rates will follow suit and also stay low during this time. Presently, the Fed is also targeting longer-term interest rates by buying mortgage-backed and commercial bonds as an insurance policy, in that regard.

Extended periods of time with very low interest rates is not good for savers. Passbook savings accounts, money market funds, and CDs are all losers in this environment. Stock, then, is the best place to be. When the Fed finally does start to raise interest rates, it is fairly likely (but not definite) that the other five Sell Rules will also indicate a stock sale should take place in the SSA portfolio. Again, all six of the Sell Rules (Chart 4) must apply before a partial sale takes place. By the way, remember that all sales within the SSA Strategy are partial; never total. And these stock sales are only meant to reestablish the investor's personal stock/bond-cash ratio. We are never 100% in bonds or cash!

Sell Rule 4 frequently anticipates rule number three. Rule 4 states: "Inflation must have exceeded 2.75% on average by year-end. When the inflation figure reaches this average at year-end, Fed tightening will either have already started or will probably soon be forthcoming. This is a good way, short of a Federal Reserve announcement to anticipate imminent Fed tightening.

Sell Rule 5 states: "The Buy Rules always trump the Sell Rules." This is pretty straight forward. It is possible that economic conditions at the end of the year could be such as to trigger all five Buy Rules as well as all six Sell Rules. Possible, but not too likely. If this were to occur, then buy, don't sell! It's more important to buy stock on sale at this time, than to reestablish the initial stock/bond-cash ratio. If all the Sell Rules still apply the following year-end, sell then.

Sell Rule 6 states: "If the Federal Reserve raises interest rates past 2% at any point during the year, and all other five Sell Rules are also triggered, then sell immediately! Do not wait until year-end. In all other cases regarding Fed actions on interest rates leading to 2% or below at year-end, this Rule 6 agrees with all other five Sell Rules" and is considered triggered when those five are also triggered. As emphasized above, "don't fight the Fed." The above Rule 6 is the one exception to year-end selling.

To summarize: we need all six of the Sell Rules in Chart 10 to apply before any selling takes place. If all six rules indicate sell, then we would sell using our predetermined stock/bond-cash portfolio ratio to reestablish this ratio.

STEP 6: MAINTAIN YOUR REESTABLISHED STOCK/BOND-CASH RATIO UNTIL THE NEXT STOCK MARKET CRASH OR CORRECTION (determined at year-end)

The purpose of this step is to reemphasize the importance of staying patient until the next stock market correction or crash. Don't be in a hurry to buy or sell until the rules dictate either action. This may very well mean waiting several years or longer during a trendless market before any action is taken. That's okay; the asset allocation of your portfolio will offer some stability and profit regardless during those times. That stability will come in the form of dividends, interest received, and internal rebalancing while you wait. Don't be tempted to "do something," regardless. The profit potential of the Strategic Stock Accumulation Strategy depends totally on waiting until those times in which the Buy/Sell Rules are triggered.

Here is a very interesting and pertinent fact: if an investor was able to follow the SSA Strategy system between 1972 and 2013, he would have made only six year-end stock purchases, and only two year-end stock sales (as would have been indicated in Chart 5) during that entire 41 year time period! (See Tables, as indicated in Chapter 9).

Remember this fact while waiting for either the Buy or Sell Rules to be triggered. Patience is key!

From time to time, it will be tempting to take some kind of buy or sell action. Don't, unless the Buy or Sell Rules dictate doing so. Remember, you have time and strategy on your side. Keep in mind that the long-term trend of the stock market is up, because of inflation and corporate profits. The inflation probably won't help a lot, but the corporate profits will. Having said that, there are times when inflation may indeed help by causing the Fed to raise interest rates. If the Fed continues to raise rates, this could very well contribute to a drop in the stock market.

This stock market drop could put large parts of the market "on sale." When the sale is then taken advantage of with SSA Strategy buying, the investor wins in two ways: 1) he buys stock at lower prices, and 2) the inflation caused market drop is eventually countered by corporate price rises (to compensate for the inflation). The investor profits by buying an artificial cheapening of stock that is subsequently corrected, leading at some point to higher stock prices down the road. These higher stock prices due to inflation will occur independent (but at the same time) of the stock market rise due to corporate profits.

It's important to try to get used to thinking counter-intuitively, because that is the basis for Strategic Stock Accumulation. And an important part of that strategy is staying cool (no fear), when things get hot (and no greed). Just wait for the right time by following the rules of SSA.

I want to end this chapter with an admonition once more, not to sell as the stock market drops during a crash or correction. I realize psychologically, this reaction can be a very difficult challenge for many people to avoid. As the stock market continues to drop during a severe stock market crash, it is tempting to throw all rationality out the window, and let fear take over. Some may feel like they are about to lose everything, as this regular stock market drop takes place (on average, once every four years). I'm not a psychologist and I don't know how to help overcome this natural human fear. And, to some extent, this fear is probably good. All I can say, <u>is if you feel in your gut there is no</u>

way you can follow the Strategic Stock Accumulation strategy, and continue buying stock as the market continues to drop, then don't even start.

If you do start the SSA strategy, by setting up the asset allocation recommended in chapters 6 and 7, then find it impossible to follow through by buying stock during a market crash or correction, then at least maintain your stock/bond-cash ratio, and at least rebalance that periodically. But don't sell stock index funds as the market drops, even though you find it impossible to buy. At least by not selling as the market drops, you will not lose forever, what you thought you lost (on paper), as subsequent retracing of the market back to pre-crash levels takes place, as it inevitably will.

I hope that the history of the stock market I have tried to emphasize, as well as the economic backdrop of free-market capitalism it operates in, will give you the confidence to not succumb to panic selling as future stock market activity simply takes its course. This future course will definitely include stock market crashes and corrections, as the night follows the day. The only question is when they will occur. Try to keep foremost in mind that the stock market always comes back. I have tried to show, as best I can, how this normal stock market activity can be taken advantage of. I hope that I have succeeded.

You must remember that if a stock market crash takes the S&P 500 down 50% or more, then you will be 100% invested in the stock market at that point. You will have no more cash in your portfolio (i.e., it will be all-stock). Your portfolio value, at that point, could be down by as much as 40% to 50% or more. However, the magnificent irony of this apparent catastrophe is that very large profits rise like the phoenix out of the ashes of its predecessor. And then you will look, and feel, like a genius! Not like all the other "geniuses" who kept buying as the market kept rising, but one who has bucked the system, so to speak, and profited accordingly. You will have won back all that you thought you had lost and then a lot more!

Now having said all of the above, I will make one final SSA Strategy suggestion: If you feel that you cannot go to a

100% stock position, as you will by following the SSA Strategy during a 50%-or-more crash, then simply resolve never to go to less than a 20–25% bond-cash position. In other words, when you have bought stock index funds during a stock market crash or correction, just stop buying, regardless of how far the market retreats from that point when your bond-cash position reaches 20–25%. Older and/or retired investors could decide on maintaining an even higher minimum cash-bond position. This will limit your gains during the subsequent market retracing, but at least you will still have bought some stock "on sale." You could then reestablish your stock/bond-cash ratio whenever the Sell Rules are triggered. You would continue to internally rebalance your portfolio as described. Then, you would wait until the next market crash or correction and follow the same strategy, stopping all stock index fund buying at somewhere between a 20%–25% bond-cash level.

The more passive approach, as mentioned above (if you find that you simply can't buy at all as the stock market is dropping) is to simply maintain your stock/bond-cash ratio as the market drops, rebalancing internally as described.

I hope that I have shown the profit potential of the Strategic Stock Accumulation Strategy to as many investors as possible, followed in its entirety. More important, I hope that all those investors, if at all possible, will be able to take advantage of it.

CHAPTER 9: Back-Testing Three Strategies, Including SSA, Back to 1929

Now, let's compare the three strategies: Proportional Rebalancing (PR), a 100% All-Stock (AS) portfolio, and Strategic Stock Accumulation (SSA), through six different time periods, ranging from 1929 to 2013. You will be able to see on a year-by-year basis, within the time periods back-tested, just how each strategy performed. You will be able to see these results on a total nominal return (inflation included) and on an inflation-adjusted real return basis. The time periods examined are not in a time-sequenced order, as it seemed more timely to look first at a period more closely associated with our present economic situation, than, for example, all the financial chaos experienced with the "Great Depression" of the 1930s. Of course, the "Great Recession" (2008–2009) of our own time had to seem comparable to many who lost over half their total assets as a result. The first time period we will examine is 2006–2013.

I've tried to make the tables and charts as easy to follow as possible. However, it would still be helpful to reread several of the paragraphs explaining how they are set up. The Charts, 1 through 9, were put within their related chapters.

The tables include a large amount of information. So

much so, in fact, that it was virtually impossible to include it all in this book in such a way as to make it readable (don't worry, you will still have complete access to it). Let me explain why: As mentioned in the Preface, it required over 300 hours minimum to accumulate, through testing, compilation, and organizing the results individually so as to make them easily understood. **There are forty-two different tables**, divided into six time periods, and seven tables per time period. The seven tables were necessary to show results of three different strategies, two of which were tested with three different stock/bond-cash ratios each (the 100% All-Stock portfolio, of course, had only one stock/bond-cash ratio). Each table required sixteen (16) columns of information, ranging from initial year-end closing S&P 500 levels to final values for all three strategies (two of which were tested in all six time periods with three different stock/bond-cash ratios). The main problem with including all this information on the pages of a book is that to include all sixteen columns <u>of only one table</u>, would require the figures to be so small as to be virtually unreadable.

This all resulted in a kind of good news/bad news scenario. The good news is that the information, in terms of final results, is as complete as I could possibly make it. I'm confident you will agree with this assessment after examining those results. The bad news is that, due to the size of the final total compiled results, I was forced to make them available on a different digital platform, a website initially set up exclusively for this purpose. The tables are easily downloadable, can be printed out, and are easily increased in size when viewed on a computer, tablet, or smartphone, to make them very clear and readable. This size modification, of course, was not possible in this book. Due to the number of columns in each table (16), the figures would simply have been too small to see.

Since its initial setup, I have expanded the site and added additional information I hope is helpful to the Strategic Stock Accumulation investor. There is now a section devoted to answering frequently asked questions about the SSA strategy, as well as other information I think investors will find helpful. The website address is http://www.stephenrperry.com. The password to retrieve and/or download, and print out the files with all compiled results is SSA2014 (SSA must be in capitals).

The procedure to follow from this point is to go to the website, use the password to bring up the backtested results, and follow along as I explain in this chapter, the relevance of the information included in each column of each table. I will only need to explain how one table is set up, since this will show how all forty-two tables are setup.

2006–2013

First, let's look at how Tables 1A through 6G are set up (see all of them in the Tables file at the website: http://www.stephenrperry.com, or simply stephenrperry.com, password: SSA2014. They are listed as follows in the Tables section: Every time period has seven tables; three for Strategic Stock Accumulation, three for Proportional Rebalancing, and one for the 100% All-Stock portfolio. The three tables for SSA and PR both are comprised of the three ratios back-tested (65/35, 50/50, and 35/65). Since the All-Stock portfolio has only one ratio, 100%/0%, it has only one table. The tables are listed as follows:

For the time period 2006–2013 (see tables 1A through 1G), Table 1, Strategic Stock Accumulation—65/35 stock/bond-cash ratio is listed as Table 1A, 50/50 stock/bond-cash ratio is 1B, and 35/65 stock/bond-cash ratio is 1C. Proportional Rebalancing—65/35 stock/bond-cash ratio is listed as 1D, 50/50 stock/bond-cash ratio is 1E, and 35/65 stock/bond-cash ratio is 1F. The 100% All-Stock—100/0 stock/bond-cash ratio is listed as 1G.

Tables 2 through 6 are structured the same way for each time period tested, so that all these other tables are in the following listed sequence:

Time Period Tested	Strategy	Table number/letter designation
2006–2013	SSA	1A-1C
	PR	1D-1F
	AS	1G
1999–2006	SSA	2A-2C
	PR	2D-2F
	AS	2G
1972–1988	SSA	3A-3C
	PR	3D-3F
	AS	3G
1929–1939	SSA	4A-4C
	PR	4D-4F
	AS	4G
1972–1999	SSA	5A-5C
	PR	5D-5F
	AS	5G
1972–2013	SSA	6A-6C
	PR	6D-6F
	AS	6G

These tables show, in detail, the comparison between the three strategies over six different time periods, the earliest beginning in 1929 and the latest ending in 2013. We start with the 2006 year-end through the 2013 year-end, the most recent time period tested which investors will be familiar with. Table 1 shows the first comparison between SSA (Strategic Stock Accumulation), PR (Proportional Rebalancing), and AS (100% All-Stock) portfolios for the year-endings of 2006 through 2013.

Let's look at how a $100,000 portfolio that is 50/50 stock/bonds-cash initial asset allocation is set up for SSA and PR (The 100% AS portfolio will always be 100% stock, and therefore have only one stock/bond-cash ratio: 100/0). Column letters have been placed at the top of all tables. The first column (A) lists the successive years within the time period tested. Column B lists the year-end prices for the S&P 500—2006 through 2013. Column C shows the change in the S&P 500, as it occurred on a cumulative basis, between 2006 and 2013, all year-end. Column D shows the percentage change in the S&P 500 on a year-by-year basis, not cumulative, but for that year only! By the way, this Column is an example (one-year change only) of what we would use to determine buy and sell decisions for the SSA strategy, based on the Buy/Sell Rules of Charts 3 and 4.

Column E indicates how the stock portion of the portfolio fared by year-end before any dividends were added. Column F shows the average dividends declared for each year for the S&P 500. In Column G, we have the post-dividend stock values.

I have added the dividends at the end of each year. In reality, of course, part of the dividends would be added during the year. This would give the ending values a slightly higher number, had they been added in that way. However, year-end makes it simple and it is used for all three strategies tested—SSA, PR, and the AS (100% All-Stock portfolio). Thus, we are comparing apples with apples, so dividend treatment will have no effect on final comparison returns. Also, we are not including expense ratios, or taxes, in the back-tested figures.

I would strongly recommend buying very low-cost index funds, as recommended earlier, such as Vanguard's S&P 500 index fund, which has an expense ratio of 0.05% (that's 5/100's of 1%). The expense ratio fee is the management fee charged to manage the fund. Since index funds track a recognized stock market index in most cases, almost no management oversight is necessary. Therefore, expense ratio fees can be kept at rock bottom levels. In spite of this fact, some brokerage firms will still charge a ridiculous fee. Use Vanguard discount brokerage as the yardstick of comparison with other discount brokerage firms.

Column H lists the amount of additional stock purchase or sale. In the case of SSA, the added stock purchases were based on the Pyramid Buying Strategy of Chart 5. For PR, the stock purchases and sales were be dependent upon maintaining the initial stock/bonds-cash ratio by buying or selling stock at every year-end in order to reestablish the beginning ratio. Taxes were impossible to determine across the board, considering the difference in investor tax rates.

As far as Strategic Stock Accumulation is concerned, tax-sheltered vehicles (such as 401[k]s or IRAs) should always be used to the greatest extent possible (or in just about any investment strategy, for that matter).

So, for example, if as in Table 1E (Proportional Rebalancing), the stock market drops 37.2% by year-end 2008, then $9349 must be shifted from the bond-cash total to the stock total by buying that much stock to reestablish the 50/50 ratio again (Column H). This resulted in a new stock/bonds-cash portfolio of $42,306 in each portion (stock and bonds-cash, Columns I and K) for a total nominal portfolio value of $84,612 (Column L). The three-month T-bill column interest figures (Column J) must be added to the bond portion before the $9349 is shifted for stock purchases.

I used the three-month U.S. T-bill interest rate for both strategies to determine how the bond-cash part of the portfolio would be affected by short-term interest rates (AS had no bond-cash portion, as it is always 100% invested in stock index funds). U.S. bonds are considered totally risk-free, as far as default is concerned. Interest rate risk is another matter. U. S. government bonds can still lose market value as interest rates rise. That is why we only use short-term government bonds in the SSA strategy. The shorter the duration, the less the bond risk.

The U.S. T-Bill short-term interest results were compared within both SSA and PR strategies. It was important for the bond portion to be turned to cash quickly both for SSA, and PR, in order to buy stock index funds when both strategy rules called for it. Short-term government bonds fit the bill. The 3-month T-Bill rate was irrelevant to the AS Strategy, since no part of that portfolio was ever invested in bonds (or cash).

Again, I simply multiplied the three-month T-bill year-end interest rates times the bond-cash balance before any rebalancing occurred at year-end. As with dividends, it is true that there would be some interest income received during the year, having a small cumulative effect by year-end. Column K shows the New Bond-Cash Total after adjusting for T-bill interest and rebalancing. Again, for simplicity and making an apples-to-apples comparison, it was done this way for both strategies. This means, if anything, that the final portfolio returns shown are slightly conservative, as long as expense ratios (within the SSA Strategy) are kept super-low by using a super-low discount brokerage firm, such as Vanguard (full disclosure: I am a Vanguard customer).

Column L shows the new total stock/bond-cash nominal portfolio value (termed on Table as "New Portfolio Value") at year-end, after any new stock was purchased or sold, and the bond-cash portion was adjusted for T-bill interest. In the case of Proportional Rebalancing, the portfolio was rebalanced to 50/50. In the case of Strategic Stock Accumulation, any rebalancing was dictated by the Buy/Sell Rules of SSA (Charts 3 and 4, Chapter 8).

I assumed for purposes of the back-testing that the entire bond-cash part of the portfolio was invested in these three-month T-bills and none in cash. Again, the apples-to-apples comparison makes this bond exclusivity irrelevant to final comparison results. This simplifies, and also, any money kept in a money market fund would receive interest very similar to the 3 month T-bill rate. On the other hand, both asset allocations, A and B, within the SSA strategy described in Chapter 8, does require certain percentages kept in cash (e.g., money market funds).

The CPI, consumer price index (Column M), toward the right of the table shows the annual year-end consumer price changes. This is a very often overlooked factor in comparing year-to-year stock market returns. By 2013, the dollar was worth 86 1/2 cents compared to year-end 2006. This represents an inflation rate of 1.93%, on average, per year. That's not really bad, as it is within the Fed's target inflation range of 2–2 1/2%. On the other hand, by 1981, the dollar was worth $0.45 as compared to 1972, so a $100,000 portfolio in 1972 was worth $45,000 in 1981 dollars (Chart 7, inflation-1972-2013). That's an inflation rate of over 6% per year, on average. During the Great Depression, on the other hand, the effect of deflation increased the value of stock 25% by 1932 year-end from its 1930 year-end value (Chart 8, inflation-1929-1939). This fact is almost never mentioned in the financial media when they discuss stock market results during "The Depression."

Today, deflation is much less likely in the US. The Federal Reserve has become too good at providing "instant" liquidity, when deemed necessary. This of course, takes the form of billions of extra printed dollars injected into the economy, through the banking system. The column immediately to the right of the CPI, Column N, shows the year-by-year consumer price change factor in the value of a portfolio, compared to 2006. For example, in 2011, the CPI change factor for the PR portfolio was .893. This means that a dollar in 2011 was worth just 89.3 cents of a dollar in 2006.

This factor of .893 had to be multiplied times the new year-end portfolio value, to give the true value in 2006 dollars, since that is our starting point for this period's comparison of the three strategies. I did this to determine the actual, inflation-adjusted return over the period back-tested, to see how well all portfolios really did (true value) while taking inflation into account. This is called the non-nominal, or inflation-adjusted, true value.

Column O shows the Strategic Stock Accumulation (SSA), Proportional Rebalancing (PR), and 100% All-Stock (AS) CPI inflation-adjusted true values. In the example of 2011 Proportional Rebalancing (50/50 ratio portfolio), Table 1E, the ending nominal (inflation not taken into account) value was $108,229 (Column L) in the Proportional Rebalancing (PR) portfolio. After taking into account the inflation factor of .893, the true inflation-adjusted PR portfolio value (in 2006 dollars), was $96,648.

An investor, following the PR Strategy with a 50/50 stock/bond-cash ratio would have thought that he was "back to even" in 2010. He was ahead at that point, based on an ending nominal (inflation not taken into account) portfolio value of $106,336, but was not actually "back to even" until 2013 on a year-end inflation-adjusted basis, with a CPI adjusted true portfolio value of $115,256.

The final column, P, indicates the year-end P/E-10 value of the S&P 500. This is not a factor in determining buy and sell decisions in the PR Strategy, since the buy/sell decisions, as well as rebalancing in that strategy, are based on year-end stock market price changes only. Nor is it a factor in the AS Strategy, since that portfolio is 100% stock at all times, regardless. It is definitely a factor in the SSA Strategy, as described in rule number 2 of the Sell Rules of Chart 4.

All 16 columns, A through P, were used to compare the 3 strategies: PR, SSA, and AS portfolio, through the 6 different time periods as shown in Tables 1(A-G) through 6 (A-G).

Again, memorize the Buy and Sell Rules of Charts 3 and 4; this will pay off "BIG-TIME!" This was made very clear by these back-tested results.

As can be seen in table 1B, the SSA 50/50 ratio chart shows a stock purchase of $28,487 at year-end 2008. In this back-tested example, the investor bought only S&P 500 stock index funds, when the buy rules called for a stock purchase. However, the SSA strategy described in Chapter 8 would require the SSA investor to buy stock index funds in such a manner as to reestablish the equal dollar values of all stock funds in Chart 1 or 2, depending on which asset allocation the SSA investor had chosen. This multiple stock index buying process was impossible to back-test, as most of these funds did not exist during at least several of the time periods tested. It is another indication that the Strategic Stock Accumulation strategy, as outlined in Chapter 8, is even more profitable than the back-tested results indicate. This is because these back-tested results do not take into account any excess return from internal rebalancing, as would occur in the recommended SSA strategy described in Chapter 8.

The $28,487 figure above from the SSA 50/50 strategy at year-end 2008 was arrived at by multiplying the previous year's bond-cash total, $52,320 times the 2008 T-bill interest rate, 1.58%. The result was $53,147. This number was then multiplied times .536 (see Chart 5) to yield the $28, 487 figure. The .536 multiplier was used because it corresponds to the 35% decline trigger in the Pyramid Buy Levels Chart. Since the two-year decline in the S&P 500 was 40.36, that number is between 35% and 42%, hence

the 35% level multiplier (.536) is used. These figures corre-
spond to the Pyramid Buy Levels Chart (Column 1 and 6)
for a bond-cash beginning total of $50,000. This repre-
sents the amount required to purchase stock, since the
stock market at year-end 2008 was down a total of 40.36%
(2007 and 2008). The -3.17% 2007 figure was added to the
-37.2% figure to equal -40.36%. No stock was bought in
2007, because by year-end, the S&P 500 was not down at
least 7% from the previous year-end (Buy Rules, Chart 3).
Instead, this -3.17% was added to the -37.2% to yield a total
two year drop of 40.36%. This means that stock should be
bought up to and including the 35% level. Since 40.36%
does not quite reach the 42% level, that percentage multiplier of .75 corresponding to that level in the Pyramid Chart
5 would not be used to determine the amount of additional
stock bought.

This purchase of $28,487 from our initial bond-cash
total of $50,000, made all the difference in our final CPI
adjusted true overall portfolio value of $144,656 (50/50
ratio) by year-end 2013. The nominal figure for SSA was
$167,232. In other words, that's how many actual 2013 dol-
lars resulted from using the SSA Strategy. The 50/50
stock/bond-cash ratio Proportional Rebalancing (Table 1E)
method, on the other hand, yielded a final CPI adjusted
value of $115,256, 25.5% lower than SSA.

An important point to consider, regarding Column 16, is
that if stock market purchase and sell decisions were made
exclusively based on P/E-10 index valuation, as many
financial advisers were recommending, then no stock at all
would have been held or bought after 2008, as in every
year since then the P/E-10 ratio has exceeded 20. Those
investors following that advice would have missed one of
the most profitable bull markets in history. This means that
they would not have recouped money lost in the 2008–
2009 bear market.

Many financial advisers consider the P/E- 10 ratio of 18
or more to indicate overvaluation. We can see here that
selling stock in the SSA Strategy does not depend solely on
P/E-10 but on all six rules listed in Chart 4 indicating and
then triggering a "Sell."

2007–2009 Stock Market Crash

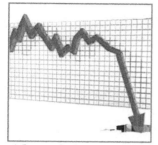

The 2007–2009 stock market crash resulted in the worst recession since the 1930s. Many people saw the value of their 401(k)s and houses cut in half or worse. Banks as usual were blamed, but there was definitely enough blame to go around—from politicians who strongly pushed the idea of almost everyone being able to own their own home, whether they could afford it or not, to many banks that were only too happy to oblige, often under pressure from those politicians, to the ratings agencies that routinely gave AAA ratings to bundled home loans sold as bonds.

With a AAA bond rating, these so-called "derivatives" were eagerly bought up by investors. As more and more homeowners defaulted on their mortgage payments, these "bonds" stopped paying interest. The housing and stock market collapse began. Many of those people who took these loans should never have had them to begin with. This group was portrayed, incorrectly or not, as the victims. Whether true or not, there was blame to be laid here also, although political correctness guided the media in other directions. Someone had to be blamed, and the politicians, of course, were not likely to blame themselves either.

As a result, those greedy bankers were once again, almost totally, the "fall guys," as they have been so many times in economic history. Of course, they were not blameless. They also got on the greed bandwagon. Hedge Funds were also somehow thrown into the mix, despite the fact they had almost nothing to do with the crash. I guess the words "hedge fund" conjures up the image of billions of dollars, so they must also be to blame. Of course, if you ask someone how the hedge funds are to blame, you are likely to get some nonsense similar to, "they're all in it with the banks."

Now the banks are requiring greater financial resources in order to buy a home. These requirements are also now mandated by law. It is simply another way for the federal government to financially repress the economy, with lower interest rates. This also makes the huge government debt easier to finance. Unfortunately, for those without jobs, it also slows down the "jobs recovery," because it slows down the recovery in general.

However, there are now, in 2014, 5% down loans available again, with supposedly adequate financial capability being demanded. So the cycle starts again, as it has so many times in the past. The takeaway from these financial fiascoes is that they have occurred and will continue to occur regularly, as a result of the human emotions of greed and fear. This will never change. Don't rail against it. Accept it as the normal byproduct of a capitalist economy. Yes, the government can act against the worst excesses with regulations and laws, but don't ever expect that to change human nature. For every law and regulation, humans, in a free-market capitalist society, will find a way to increase risk, and therefore return, regardless. Over 200 years of U.S. capitalist economic history including repeated booms and busts, says that you can count on it (and profit from it!)

Back-tested results showed that probably the most powerful factor regarding the success of SSA is the continuing volatility of the stock market. According to S&P Equity Research, "There has been 15 bear markets since 1929, the average lasting 19 months and down a stunning 40%." Not all of them led to severe market crashes, but they will still be profitable for the SSA investor. Seen in this light, the obvious question is not, "How can I avoid those stock market corrections almost every decade, on average?" but rather, "How can I best profit from them?"

Strategic Stock Accumulation will be shown to accomplish this goal, as we continue to examine six particularly severe market corrections. I will show how each performed over these individual time periods. I will show, specifically, how SSA fared by systematically buying stock as the market dropped during these times, as compared to the Proportional Rebalancing and 100% All-Stock Strategies. The results are eye-opening.

Charts 1A and 1D show stock market returns between year-end 2006 and year-end 2013 with a 65/35 stock/bonds-cash ratio for both the SSA and the PR strategies. The SSA Strategy wins out over the PR. The final (back to 2006) portfolio value of the Pyramid SSA Strategy was $162,296 (inflation-adjusted value was $140,386). For the PR, the corresponding 65/35 ratio values were $139,809 and $120,935, respectively. <u>This is a 16.1% greater final return for SSA over PR.</u> Again, this is very significant, considering that PR is now the most commonly recommended and followed investment approach by financial advisers and money managers. This strategy is also commonly referred to as "Asset Allocation" along with periodic "Rebalancing."

During the "go-go dot-com 90's," PR was rarely mentioned. For all practical purposes, this strategy did not exist. Now, almost all financial advisers talk about "rebalancing," almost exclusively, with their clients (even though the strategy shows poor results overall, as I will show clearly). I guess its appeal lies in the lower-risk that focusing on rebalancing alone affords to a portfolio, regardless of overall returns. Apparently, not much has been done in the way of effectively back-testing the strategy until now. If it previously has, the results gained in comparison with overall stock market returns must not have been impressive, if performed properly.

Table 1C shows that the final year-end 2013 (2006-2013) results for the SSA Strategy with a 35/65 stock/bonds-cash ratio was $172,580, annualized nominal return. The PR number for this same ratio (Table 1F) was $125,930. <u>This represents 37% increase return of SSA over PR.</u> The PR Strategy is simply not very profit-yielding when only a 35% stock portfolio position is risked in the market, year after year. On the other hand, as mentioned before, this does reduce investor risk. SSA, with a 35/65 ratio, retains most the profit potential of its 65/35 ratio, and also reduces the risk significantly, because large amounts of stock are bought only at low prices. Even though large amounts of the bonds-cash position are being sold to buy stock (within the 35/65 stock/bond-cash ratio portfolio), SSA is only risky if you believe the stock market will not retrace to its previous high at some point in the not too distant future. That would be a false assumption, based on almost all U.S. economic history.

Table 1G shows only the results of a 100% fully invested All-Stock portfolio. This is a high risk portfolio for older and/or retired investors. It could very well take a number of years to recover from a serious stock market crash or correction, since there is no bond or cash position to "cushion the blow." Also inflation, to a large extent, cancels out the relatively low dividends paid out on average today. This is unlike the depression years of the 1930s, when deflation and dividends (over twice what they are today) bailed out long-term investors within three to four years. A severe correction in the stock market today could temporarily devastate a 100% stock portfolio. Although this is eventually very advantageous for the SSA investor, an older investor must take his investment time limits into consideration. A 35/65 stock/bond-cash ratio fits the bill.

The exception to this recommendation would be young and middle-age investors, possibly up to age 55. They have sufficient years to recover from such a correction or crash, and in most cases, the more stock they can get their hands on from their 20s on to their mid-50's, the better their final result will be in their 60s and 70s.

During the years of 2006–2013, a 100% stock position yielded mediocre results by year-end 2013. All three stock/bonds-cash ratios of SSA strategies proved superior (see Tables 1A-C and 1G) to AS. The same cannot be said for Proportional Rebalancing. A 100% All-Stock position during this period had a final inflation-adjusted value of $130,414 by year-end 2013 (Table 1G) (but was not "back to even" at year-end 2012, finishing at $100,252). PR on the other hand, ended at $115,256 (50/50 ratio), $108,929 (35/65), and $120,935 (65/35) (Tables 1D-F), all inflation-adjusted.

Again, this does not mean an AS fully invested in stock position is, at all times, superior to annual Proportional Rebalancing (however, AS is rarely superior to Strategic Stock Accumulation—SSA). For example, from 1999–2006, PR beat AS at all three ratios (Tables 2 D-F and Table 2G). From 1972–1988, however, a fully invested (AS) in stock position (Table 3G)) resulted in a final inflation-adjusted value from 1972 to 1988 of 154,691. PR final values for the 1972–1988 period were 156,299 (65/35 ratio), $136,471 (50/50), and $141,380 (35/65) (Tables 3D-F). So, a fully invested (AS) 100% stock position (Table 3G) was superior to PR in two of the three ratios back-tested between 1972 and 1988. However, the PR Strategy was obviously much less risky, over all time periods.

The effectiveness of AS (100% stock portfolio) over the PR Strategy during the 41-year period (1972–2013) is borne out by the results shown in Table 6G and Chart 9 (Comparison of Three Strategies Through Six Time Periods). A $100,000 initial AS portfolio in 1972 (41 years later) yielded a final true (inflation-adjusted) value of $876,601 in 2013 (nominal value was $4,816,487), a CR (cumulative return) of 853.6%, and a compound annual growth rate (CAGR) of 5.66%. The CAGR of PR, on the other hand, ended at 4.38% (65/35), 3.65% (50/50), and 2.95% (35/65).

CAGR is a mathematical formula that allows for a 'smoothed' rate of return. This is also termed as the "annualized" return. It shows what an investment yields on an annually compounded basis. However, one certainly cannot assume the CAGR is achieved exactly every year. It does not show the annual ups and downs of the stock market, but instead, it shows a true overall rate of return over any time period. It allows an investor to see what he really has at the end of an investment period. Average annual return doesn't really tell you this, because an "average" is not the "true" yield. CAGR is the best way to compare how one investment performs in relation to others. The main drawback to this formula is that it gives no reflection on volatility. So it can give the impression of a steady growth rate, in spite of the fact the value of the investment can vary considerably from one year to the next.

I have used the ending CAGR for all time periods, all ratios, and all strategies tested, in addition to the overall CR (cumulative return). This CAGR is the most significant number to be used in evaluating all three strategies (Chart 9, Comparison of Three Strategies Through Six Time

Periods). While high volatility is normally considered to be a negative factor by most investors, it is actually a positive factor for the SSA investor. This is because the increased volatility is what allows more stock to be bought at lower prices ("on sale").

On a risk-adjusted basis, while PR would be preferable in most investor's minds due to its low volatility, it is actually a very limiting feature of the strategy. This is because low volatility limits the profit potential of the PR Strategy, while at the same time reducing risk. The tradeoff is not a good one, in my opinion.

Even though older investors need to limit risk, the added volatility of SSA is preferable to the limited volatility of Proportional Rebalancing, especially on a short-term basis. This is because the added volatility is what results in greater profits for the SSA investor. If a 35/65 stock/bond-cash ratio is followed, he or she can have the best of both worlds: lower volatility and higher profit potential. The so-called deep-risk (long-term), as well as short-term risk, is only important for the older, or retired investor, who may need their investment funds for living expenses before their portfolio is able to take advantage of the succeeding upward trend of the stock market after a crash or correction.

SSA is the best approach, even for younger investors (stock/bond-cash ratio of 65/35), because more stock can be purchased this way at lower prices regardless of the investor's age. This is because of the regular stock market corrections that are inevitable through almost every decade. Even though the long-term upward trend of the stock market is very likely to be profitable using an AS Strategy, for younger and middle-age investors, the periodic market crashes put these investors at risk of "bailing out" early in their investment careers, causing them to lose the benefit of the time advantage they possess during this stage of their lives. For this reason, SSA is also psychologically, as well as strategically, superior to AS at any age.

1999–2006

The year 1999 ended a period in the U.S. stock market

of the longest upward gains in its history. This remarkable time started in 1982, and the average gain was over 14% annually for 18 years! If one were lucky enough just to be fully invested over this time period, he or she would have had a truly successful long-term result by January 2000. By March 2000, however, everything started to change. Investors at this time were used to the market dropping, coming back within a short time, and then resuming its upward trajectory. Few realized that it wasn't coming back this time, for at least another three to five years. Stocks, especially new technology stocks (i.e., the so-called "dot-coms") were wildly overvalued.

Many tech stocks were valued at a price that would have taken 50 to 100 years for their profits to catch up to their price, based on P/E figures at the time. Even after this previous high was matched by year-end 2006 (S&P 500 was at 1424), the market was still overvalued by its P/E-10 ratio measure of 27.2. This is a major reason why it crashed again between 2007 and 2009. It was still overvalued in 2007 (PE-10 was at 24.01). This simple fact is often overlooked, and the market crash of 2007–2009 is often attributed to everything but simple overvaluation. It is true that a bubble existed also in the housing market, and this only exacerbated the problem. But the stock market itself was simply still overvalued from its high in 2000.

Tables 2B and 2E show the comparison between the results for SSA and PR at the 50/50 stock/bonds-cash ratio for the years between year-end 1999 and 2006. Inflation was a factor, but it was not excessive, especially compared to the 1970's (see Chart 7). PR's nominal (non-inflation-adjusted) value at that point was $119,708. The total nominal SSA 50/50 portfolio value at year-end 2006 was $139,769, representing a 16.8% increase over the Proportional Rebalancing 50/50 Strategy.

Following the buying strategy, as indicated by the Pyramid Buy Levels, Chart 5, the 50/50 stock/bond-cash ratio within the SSA Strategy would have resulted in a total of $44,585 worth of stock being bought by year-end 2002 ($11,732 in 2001 and $32,853 in 2002). The $11,732 purchase in 2001 was triggered by the stock market S&P 500 drop of 21% (total in 2000 and 2001, resulting in a stock purchase representing 21.4% of the bonds-cash portion of the portfolio), while the $32,853 bought at year-end 2002 occurred because the stock market dropped another 21.4%, making the 3 years' total of year-to-year drops equal 42.4%. This meant that 75% of the remaining bond-cash position was used to purchase stock. This figure was reached by adding -6.3% in 2000, -14.7 in 2001, and -21.4% in 2002. This resulted in the corresponding total purchase of $44,585 during year-ends 2001 and 2002, as shown in Table 2B, for the 50/50 stock/bond-cash ratio (SSA).

Tables 2C and 2F show the results from a 35/65 stock/bonds-cash ratio portfolio for both SSA and PR between the 1999 year-end and the 2006 year-end. The beginning $100,000 balance in SSA ended at a value of $148,359 nominal, but only $121.202 with the PR Strategy. So, while the SSA showed a 48.4% seven-year total return, PR returned only 21.2% (Chart 9). This represented an increased CR of 27.2% from the Strategic Stock Accumulation Strategy over the Proportional Rebalancing Strategy for that ratio (35/65) and for that time period (1999–2006).

Table 2A, at a stock/bonds-cash ratio of 65/35, resulted in a final value of $131,333 nominal ($109,006 inflation-adjusted) for the SSA Strategy and $117,772 nominal (only $97,751 inflation-adjusted) for the PR Strategy (Chart 2D). The 65/35 Strategic Stock Accumulation Strategy exceeded the corresponding PR Strategy by 11.5% during this period. So, the Proportional Rebalancing approach actually lost money over the seven-year period on an inflation-adjusted basis. The AS portfolio did worst of all during this period, ending at $111,656 nominal ($92,674 inflation-adjusted), as shown in Table 2G and in Chart 9.

1972–1988

The time period between 1972 and 1988 included inflation and stagflation in the 1970s and the beginning of the best 18 years in the history of the U.S. stock market (1982–2000). 1982–1988 is, of course, included in this period's back-testing data. I did this to show the effectiveness of

SSA and PR during an extended period of stagflation and also to show how both strategies compared for the six years (1982–1988) subsequent to that decade, as the market began to perform very well. I will also show later how both strategies fared between 1989 and 2000, all of which were very good years for the stock market.

Chart 7 (Inflation 1972–2013)

1972-2013

ANNUAL INFLATION-ADJUSTED

4.29% AVG. ANNUAL INFLATION RATIO

YEAR ENDING	CPI CHANGE	INFLATION
1972	Base Year=42.6	
1973	42.6→46.6	9.4%
1974	45.6→52.1	11.5%
1975	51.1→55.6	**6.7%**
1976	55.6→58.5	5.2%
1977	58.5→62.5	7.2%
1978	62.5→68.3	9.3%
1979	68.3→77.8	13.9%
1980	77.8→87.0	11.8%
1981	87.0→94.3	8.4%
1982	94.3→97.8	3.3%

YEAR ENDING	CPI CHANGE	INFLATION
1983	97.8→101.9	4.2%
1984	101.9→105.3	3.5%
1985	105.5→109.6	3.9%
1986	109.6→111.2	1.5%
1987	111.2→115.7	4.0%
1988	115.7→121.1	4.7%
1989	121.1→127.4	5.2%
1990	127.4→134.6	5.3%
1991	134.6→138.1	2.6%
1992	138.1→142.6	3.3%
1993	142.6→146.2	2.5%
1994	146.2→150.3	2.5%
1995	150.3→154.4	2.7%
1996	154.4→159.1	3.0%
1997	159.1→161.6	1.6%
1998	161.6→164.3	1.7%
1999	164.3→168.8	2.7%
2000	168.8→175.1	3.7%
2001	175.1→177.1	1.1%

YEAR ENDING	CPI CHANGE	INFLATION
2002	177.1→181.7	2.6%
2003	1814.7→185.2	1.9%
2004	185.2→190.7	3.0%
2005	190.7→198.3	4.0%
2006	198.3→202.416	2.1%
2007	202.416→211.08	4.3%
2008	211.08→211.143	0.02%
2009	211.143→216.687	2.6%
2010	216.687→220.223	1.6%
2011	220.223→226.665	2.9%
2012	226.665→230.28	1.6%
2013	230.28→233.916	1.5%

Chart 8 (Inflation 1929–1939)

CHART 8: 1929 – 1939 INFLATION-DEFLATION		
1929 – 1939 INFLATION/DEFLATION		
YEAR ENDING	CPI CHANGE	INFLATION/ DEFLATION
1929	0	0
1930	0	0
1931	17.1 --> 14.3	-16.4%
1932	14.3 --> 12.9	-9.8%
1933	12.9 --> 13.2	+2.3%
1934	13.2 --> 13.6	+3.0%
1935	13.6 --> 13.8	+1.5%
1936	13.8 --> 14.1	+2.2%
1937	14.1 --> 14.2	+0.7%
1938	14.2 --> 14.0	-1.4%
1939	14.0 --> 13.9	-0.7%

I was confident at the outset of this back-testing that SSA would outperform the other two strategies during times of stock market correction and crashes, but what about in extended bull markets? After all, the greatest potential for eventual profit in the SSA Strategy is during periods of market decline. These 'bull market' results were remarkable also, mainly because of the market's gyrations (volatility) that occurred regularly during the stock market booms, busts, and economic expansions. It was also during some of these times that stock could be bought at low, bargain prices, even when no extended market crash or correction may have occurred. Shorter 'bear markets' within a longer-term, so-called "secular bull market" would also occur due to normal stock market volatility.

Tables 3B and 3E show a comparison between both strategies at the 50/50 ratio. By 1988, if we include dividends, 90-day T-bill rates, and inflation, the SSA had a 1988 year-end value of $583,579 nominal ($205,420 inflation-adjusted), starting from the initial $100,000 at year-end 1972. The PR ending value was $387,702 nominal (Table 3E), and $136,471 inflation-adjusted). These results also showed a 50.5% increased return of SSA over PR for the 50/50 ratio. SSA year-end 1988 results were $194,010 inflation-adjusted for the 65/35 portfolio (Table 3A) and $156,299 for PR (65/35, Table 3D).

Table 3C shows the best results for SSA at a year-end 1988 value of $216,875 inflation-adjusted (35/60 ratio portfolio). <u>PR results were 53.4% less than SSA at $141,380, inflation-adjusted (35/65 ratio)</u>. The AS portfolio (Table 3G) was a better strategy during this time, finishing at $154,691, than was Proportional Rebalancing, at both the 50/50 ratio ($136,471) and at the 35/65 ratio ($141,380). <u>Under all three strategies back-tested, however, the AS (All-Stock portfolio) always lagged the Strategic Stock Accumulation Strategy (SSA) during this time period!</u>

Chart 9 (Comparison of Three Strategies Through Six Time Periods)

6 TIME PERIODS – STRATEGY COMPARISON (NOMINAL)

6 TIME PERIODS	100% STOCK PORT-FOLIO	STRATEGIC STOC ACCUMULATION (SSA) %			PROPORTIONAL REBALANCING %		
	A	B	C	D	E	F	G
1928-1939	100%	65/35	50/50	35/65	65/35	50/50	35/65
Begining Value	100,000	100,000	100,000	100,000	100,000	100,000	100,000
Final Value	108.835	148,631	164,175	181,079	134,120	141,030	144,595
Cumulative Return (CR)	8.8%	48.63%	64.18%	81.08%	34.1%	41.0%	44.6%
Compound Annual Growth Rate (CAGR)	0.79%	3.67%	4.61%	5.55%	2.69%	3.17%	3.44%
1972-1988	100%	65/35	50/50	35/65	65/35	50/50	35/65
Begining Value	100,000	100,000	100,000	100,000	100,000	100,000	100,000
Final Value	439,462	551,164	583,579	616,123	440,030	387,702	401,649
Cumulative Return (CR)	339.5%	451.2%	483.6%	516.1%	344.0%	287.7%	302.0%
Compound Annual Growth Rate	9.69%	11.26%	11.66%	12.04%	9.76%	8.84%	9.08%

(CAGR)							
	A	**B**	**C**	**D**	**E**	**F**	**G**
1972-1999	**100%**	**65/35**	**50/50**	**35/65**	**65/35**	**50/50**	**35/65**
Begining Value	100,000	100,000	100,000	100,000	100,000	100,000	100,000
Final Value	2,857,311	2,769,702	2,573,147	2,342,029	1,874,536	1,341,221	1,140,121
Cumulative Return (CR)	2,757.3%	2,669.7%	2,473.1%	2,242.0%	1,774.5%	1,247.2%	1,040.1%
Compound Annual Growth Rate (CAGR)	13.22%	13.09%	12.78%	12.39%	11.47%	10.11%	9.43%
1972-2013	**100%**	**65/35**	**50/50**	**35/65**	**65/35**	**50/50**	**35/65**
Begining Value	100,000	100,000	100,000	100,000	100,000	100,000	100,000
Final Value	4,816,487	5,403,298	5.,337,977	5,180,905	3,086,521	2,152,790	1,779,623
Cumulative Return (CR)	4,716.5%	5,303.3%	5,238.0%	5,080.9%	2,986.5%	2,052,.8%	1,679.5%
Compound Annual Growth Rate (CAGR)	9.91%	10.22%	10.19%	10.11%	8.72%	7.77%	7.72%
1999-2006	**100%**	**65/35**	**50/50**	**35/65**	**65/35**	**50/50**	**35/65**

Begining Value	100,000	100,000	100,000	100,000	100,000	100,000	100,000
	A	**B**	**C**	**D**	**E**	**F**	**G**
Final Value	111,656	131,333	139,769	148,359	117,722	119,708	121,202
Cumulative Return (CR)	11.7%	31.3%	39.8%	48.4%	17.8%	19.7%	21.2%
Compound Annual Growth Rate (CAGR)	1.59%	3.97%	4.90%	5.80%	2.36%	2.60%	2.79%
2006-2013	**100%**	**65/35**	**50/50**	**35/65**	**65/35**	**50/50**	**35/65**
Begining Value	100,000	100,000	100,000	100,000	100,000	100,000	100,000
Final Value	150,767	162,296	167,232	172,580	139,809	133,244	125,930
Cumulative Return (CR)	50.8%	62.3%	67.2%	72.6%	39.8%	33.2%	25.9%
Compound Annual Growth Rate (CAGR)	6.04%	7.16%	7.62%	8.11%	4.90%	4.19%	3.35%

6 TIME PERIODS – STRATEGY COMPARISON (INFLATION ADJUSTED)

6 TIME PERIODS	100% STOCK PORT- FOLIO	STRATEGIC STOC ACCUMULATION (SSA) %			PROPORTIONAL REBALANCING %		
	A	B	C	D	E	F	G
1928-1939	100%	65/35	50/50	35/65	65/35	50/50	35/65
Begining Value	100,000	100,000	100,000	100,000	100,000	100,000	100,000
Final Value	108,835	148,631	164,175	181,079	134,120	141,030	144,595
Cumulative Return (CR)	8.8%	48.63%	64.18%	81.08%	34.1%	41.04%	44.6%
Compound Annual Growth Rate (CAGR)	0.79%	3.67%	4.61%	5.55%	2.69%	3.17%	3.44%
1972-1988	100%	65/35	50/50	35/65	65/35	50/50	35/65
Begining Value	100,000	100,000	100,000	100,000	100,000	100,000	100,000
Final Value	154,691	194,010	205,420	216,875	156,299	136,471	141,380
Cumulative Return (CR)	54.7%	94.01%	105.42%	106.88%	56.3%	36.4%	41.4%
Compound Annual Growth Rate (CAGR)	2.76%	4.23%	4.60%	4.96%	2.83%	1.96%	2.19%

	A	B	C	D	E	F	G
1972-1999	**100%**	**65/35**	**50/50**	**35/65**	**65/35**	**50/50**	**35/65**
Begining Value	100,000	100,000	100,000	100,000	100,000	100,000	100,000
Final Value	720,114	697,965	648,433	590,191	472,383	339,500	287,311
Cumulative Return (CR)	620.1%	597.97%	548.43%	490.19	372.4%	239.5%	187.3%
Compound Annual Growth Rate (CAGR)	7.59%	7.46%	7.17%	6.80%	5.92%	4.63%	3.99%
1972-2013	**100%**	**65/35**	**50/50**	**35/65**	**65/35**	**50/50**	**35/65**
Begining Value	100,000	100,000	100,000	100,000	100,000	100,000	100,000
Final Value	876,601	983,400	971,512	942,925	561,747	391,808	323,892
Cumulative Return (CR)	776.5%	883.4%	871.5%	842.93%	461.75%	291.8%	223.9%
Compound Annual Growth Rate (CAGR)	5.44%	5.73%	5.70%	5.63%	4.30%	3.39%	2.91%

	A	B	C	D	E	F	G
1999-2006	**100%**	**65/35**	**50/50**	**35/65**	**65/35**	**50/50**	**35/65**
Final Value	92,674	109,006	116,008	123,138	97,751	99,358	100,598
Cumulative Return (CR)	-7.33%	9.01%	16.01%	23.1%	-2.25%	-0.064%	0.06%
Compound Annual Growth Rate (CAGR)	-1.10%	1.24%	2.14%	3.02%	-0.002%	-0.09%	0.085%
2006-2013	**100%**	**65/35**	**50/50**	**35/65**	**65/35**	**50/50**	**35/65**
Begining Value	100,000	100,000	100,000	100,000	100,000	100,000	100,000
Final Value	130.414	140,386	144,656	147,728	120,935	115,256	108,920
Cumulative Return (CR)	30.4%	40.39%	44.66%	47.73%	20.9%	15.3%	8.9%
Compound Annual Growth Rate (CAGR)	3.87%	4.97%	5.42%	5.73%	2.76%	2.05%	1.24%

Cumulative Return (CR) =

$$\frac{\text{(Current Price of Security)} - \text{(Original Price of Security)}}{\text{(Original Price of Security)}}$$

Compound Annual Growth Rate (CAGR) =

$$CAGR = \left(\frac{\text{Ending Value}}{\text{Beginning Value}} \right)^{\left(\frac{1}{\text{\# of years}} \right)} - 1$$

1928–1939

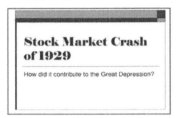

The 1928–1939 time period was truly disastrous for most Americans and for many people worldwide, for that matter. It began with the so-called 'Great Depression' and culminated in the beginning of the Second World War. During this time, the unemployment rate reached 25% in the U.S. The stock market crash in this country also resulted in the unemployment of millions of people across the globe. The crash began in the U.S. and spread to Europe soon after.

Under the same circumstances if experienced today, the crash would not have happened. Aside from finally lowering interest rates, the Fed at that time stood by and did virtually nothing. In its defense, this was considered appropriate financial policy for a central bank at the time. They clearly did not know what to do! The majority of stock owned on the New York Stock Exchange was bought by investors and speculators with borrowed money, so that when the stock market began to drop, this borrowed money was called in by the banks and brokerages in the form of loan repayment demands and margin calls.

Investors (many were speculators) were forced to sell most of their stock, speeding up crash momentum. As a result, people began to take their money out of the banks. Banks could not meet all of these withdrawal demands, and thousands failed.

People lost their life savings, as bank failures continued to multiply. There was no unemployment compensation, so people who were all of the sudden out of work had no income whatsoever. To make matters much worse, during this time, giant dust storms began in the Midwest farm belt, which destroyed crops and caused financial devastation for farmers. With no crops, and therefore no income, thousands of farmers were forced off their farms through foreclosure. John Steinbeck's *The Grapes of Wrath* describes the misery of these people, as large numbers of them traveled west to work under almost inhumane conditions as virtual slaves in the California grape fields. Hard to believe, but this actually happened in this country.

The Federal Reserve today has much more experience dealing with recessions and stock market crashes. It knows very well and is now able (unlike in the 1930's) to provide instant liquidity to the markets, which was not even attempted in the early 1930s (due in large part to the limitations imposed upon it by the "gold standard"). Today, we have the FDIC, which insures most bank deposits against bank failure. There is unemployment insurance to help mitigate the worst effects of unemployment. Workers Compensation insurance today deals with on-the-job injuries. We have Social Security, Medicaid, and other various forms of government social "safety nets," none of which existed in the 1930s, during the "Depression," as it was widely termed even at that time. Also, most important today, there is now no "gold standard" to tie the hands of the Fed.

However, again to compare "apples with apples," and to back-test SSA, PR, and AS, I will test how all three strategies would have performed during this tragic time.

It is important to reemphasize that there were two other conditions existing during the 1930s that are not present today in the U.S.: deflation and relatively (as compared to today) large dividend payments. This meant that if an investor did not use borrowed money to buy stock up to the beginning of the crash in October 1929 and held on to that stock without selling, he was actually made whole by 1935 on a deflation-adjusted basis (by including dividends and the effects of deflation). This is a far cry from the often-repeated mistake in the financial media, which dates the stock market recovery from the beginning of the Depression in 1929, all the way to 1954. Why is this? Simply because those dividends and deflation are not included in the 1954 calculation. Dividends averaged between 5% and 6% during this time and less than 2% today!

Between 1929 and 1932, the dollar gained 32.6% because of deflation. Prices plummeted, because people had very little money to buy goods and services. This meant that $100 in 1929 could buy $132.60 worth of those same goods and services by 1932 (in 1929 dollars), if one had the money to buy goods and services. This fact, together with an average 5.4% compounded annual dividend, meant investor financial recovery was much faster than is widely believed. This assumes, of course, that the investor did not sell any stock during this time (a big assumption in most cases).

Table 4G, and Chart 9, shows the AS portfolio of such an investor in an S&P 500 modeled portfolio had $108,835 deflation adjusted by year-end 1939. This was in spite of a 35.7% drop in the stock market in 1937. However, the SSA 50/50 ratio portfolio (Table 4B), on the other hand, ended at an impressive $164,175 in 1939. The 35/65 portfolio (Table 4C) finished at an astounding $181,079, and the 65/35 portfolio (Table 4A and Chart 9) finished at $148,631. All of these figures were deflation-adjusted and occurred during what many believed was the worst financial disaster in American history. The corresponding PR results were: the 50/50 portfolio (Table 4E and Chart 9) yielded $141,030; 35/65 (Table 4 F and Chart 9) ended at $144,595; and 65/35 (Table 4D and Chart 9) finished at $134,120; all deflation-adjusted. The 35/65 Strategic Stock Portfolio out returned an AS portfolio during this period by 66.4%.

1972–1999

The years between 1972 and 2000 (year-end 1999) were excellent for an AS portfolio and for an SSA investor. They were mediocre for the PR Strategy. This was in spite of the fact that between 1988 and year-end 1999, there were only 2 year-end S&P 500 declines: -4.26 in 1990 and -1.64% in 1994 (all in Table 5-A through G). The CR (cumulative return) for AS between 1972 and 1999 was 620.1%, inflation-adjusted, with a CAGR (compound annual growth rate) of 7.59% (Chart 9). This shows the overall power of a fully invested (AS) position in a strong, extended bull market. The SSA Strategy, however, was not far behind during this time period, in all three ratios and with much less risk (see Tables 5A-C and Chart 9).

The 65/35 ratio (in Chart 9) of the SSA portfolio gained 598.0% on a cumulative basis inflation-adjusted, with a CAGR of 7.46%. The AS portfolio CAGR was 1.7% higher than SSA during this period, also inflation-adjusted. The 50/50 portfolio finished at 548.4% CR (cumulative return) and 7.17% CAGR. The 35/65 SSA portfolio ended up 490.2% CR and 6.80% CAGR (Charts 9). So, even though the 1990s was fantastic for the stock market, with few opportunities to buy large amounts of stock at "bargain basement" prices, the SSA portfolio did very well, with substantial cash positions for most of that time, resulting in much less risk. Proportional Rebalancing, again, trailed the others. PR resulted in a 65/35 ratio return of 372.4% CR and 5.92% CAGR; a 50/50 ratio return of 239.5% CR and 4.63% CAGR; and a 35/65 ratio return of 187.3% CR and 3.99% CAGR (all in Chart 9). The final 65/35 stock/bond-cash Strategic Stock Accumulation value was $2,769,702 nominal! The corresponding PR ratio final value was $1,874,536. This represented a 47.8% higher return of SSA over PR for that ratio and that time period. SSA final value returns for the 50/50 and 35/65 ratios exceeded those of PR ratios by 91% and 105.4%, respectively!

These results strongly indicate that PR may only be appropriate for an older investor or retiree, satisfied with a low risk but lower return portfolio. This is appropriate for risk-averse investors in that age group but not for any younger investors seeking at least market-matching long-term capital growth. Older investors can do a lot better with less risk by following a 35/65 stock/bond-cash ratio SSA Strategy.

1972–2013

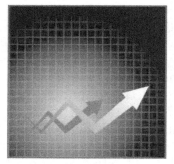

The 1972–2013 period covers the largest time range—41 years. This gives the investor an excellent comparison as to how all three strategies performed over a longer timeframe.

1972–2013 covers at least four bull markets and three stock market crashes. It includes a time period when the Federal Reserve did not handle inflation or liquidity well, allowing both to reach levels difficult for it to control (between the mid-70s to 1981). From 1982 to the present, the Fed did much better, but still allowed interest rates to stay too low (in the 1990s), probably contributing to the "bubble-like" condition of the stock market by the late 90s.

Having talked about all of the above earlier, the necessary actions of the Federal Reserve are always second-guessed, right or wrong. There are regular calls to limit the independence of the Fed. This frequently takes the form of demands to "audit the Fed" (by those who blame it for the nation's debt problems), for an "easy money" policy, or a "too tight" money policy. The blame for the U.S. debt, however, lies solely with the U.S. Congress, not with the Federal Reserve. Congress makes the laws and has the "power of the purse." The ability of the Federal Reserve to control monetary policy (interest rates and money supply) is vitally important to compensate for the U. S. Congress' present inability to implement effective fiscal policy (borrowing and spending). Limiting the Fed's independence would be a mistake. As soon as the Federal Reserve comes under control of the politicians, these government "leaders" would start pandering to their voting constituencies, destroying the effectiveness of the Federal Reserve. This would present many problems, since the Federal Reserve, as explained further in Chapter 3, does serve a vitally important function in our economy.

Regardless of what the Fed does or doesn't do, the stock

market will always overreach on both the high and low side. After either market direction (up or down), it will eventually mean revert in an attempt to right itself (because of investor reaction). So, don't get "hung up" on the actions of the Fed. Just accept the stock market on its own terms. Just because the Fed may have erred in its policy actions, at this time or that, doesn't make a bit of difference as far as your ability to make money in the stock market. I'm simply discussing government economic policy, not anything you should base your buying and selling decisions on. Base those decisions on the strategy of Strategic Stock Accumulation.

The 1972-2013 time period also included when President Richard Nixon took gold completely out of the equation by no longer even allowing other countries to help control their currency values by demanding our gold in exchange for dollars. Individual investors had not been allowed to own gold since 1934. The 1970s included years of very high inflation, and toward the end, very high interest rates. The period between 2000 and 2013, on the other hand, saw relatively lower inflation and interest rates. The U.S. was involved in four wars from 1972 to 2013: Vietnam, Desert Storm 1, and Desert Storm 2, and Afghanistan, and also, significant NATO military action in Bosnia. Economically, the Great Recession of 2008–2009 was second in economic calamity only to the Great Depression of the 1930s.

This time included some of the scariest moments of the Cold War involving the U.S. and the Soviet Union, as well as the relative calm after the breakup of the Soviet Union. It also included the slow rise of China as a stronger economic power. Thankfully, one serious event that, as of yet, has not occurred, is total (or even limited) nuclear war. At any rate, we must make investment decisions based on what is happening, not on what might have happened or may happen.

1972–2013 included many different world events that, in one way or another, buffeted the stock market, at least temporarily. It is, therefore, an excellent economic and financial milieu in which to back-test these three stock market strategies.

Reverting back to year-end 1999, for example, the AS inflation-adjusted real value was $720,114 (Table 5G and Chart 9, Column A). The 65/35 ratio SSA portfolio ended in 1999 at $697,965 inflation-adjusted (Table 5A, and Chart 9, Column B). However, the AS portfolio was down to $413,113 at year-end 2008 (Table 6G), while the 50/50 SSA portfolio (Table 6C) finished that year (2008) at $475,607, inflation-adjusted. The Proportional Rebalancing portfolio (50/50) finished at a not very impressive $275,654 (Table 6F). By year-end 2013, the AS (Table 6G, Chart 9, Column A) finished the 41-year period at $876,601, inflation-adjusted to 1972.

All 3 strategies started 1972 with a $100,000 portfolio. The CR for the AS portfolio was 776.6% nominal and the CAGR was 5.44% (Chart 9, Column B). The 65/35 stock/bond-cash SSA ratio portfolio exceeded the 100% All-Stock portfolio return starting in 1972 and continuing to 2013—41 years! This additional final inflation-adjusted total of SSA over AS was 12.2%, representing the most significant result for all the years back-tested. By the end of 2013, the 65/35 SSA portfolio was up cumulatively 5303.3% with a 10.22% CAGR (Chart 9, Column B) holding a final value of $5,403,298 ($983,400 inflation-adjusted). The SSA 50/50 ratio ended at 5238.0% cumulatively, with a CAGR of 10.19% (Chart 9, Column C), and a final overall value of $5,337,977 ($971,512 inflation-adjusted). The 35/65 SSA ended at a value of $5,180,905 ($942,925 inflation-adjusted), a CAGR of 10.11%, and a final CR of 5080.9%. All of these SSA returns are based on historical S&P 500 results and would have been realized without internal rebalancing. Internal rebalancing, as explained previously, would have increased the final returns of SSA over and above those included here and will have a positive effect on the returns of the Strategic Stock Accumulation Strategy in going forward.

This additive rebalancing effect within SSA should result conservatively, in at least a 30-35% additional return over an investment lifetime (period of 30-40 years). How do I estimate this figure? 0.75% to 1% additional return from rebalancing per year compounded, I think, is very reasonable. Over a 30-to-40-year investment career, this compounding effect could easily lead to a more than 30-35 percent final value. This, in itself, would represent a very large additional final value!

If rebalancing is so effective, you may be wondering, within the SSA Strategy, why were the PR (proportional rebalancing) results overall, through all time periods tested, so unimpressive? This is because PR Strategy dictates that rebalancing be done every year primarily at the level of the overall stock/bond-cash ratio. This means that every year in which the stock market shows a gain, stock is then sold within the stock portion of the portfolio and moved to the bond-cash portion, limiting future returns from stock market gains.

The Strategic Stock Accumulation, on the other hand, does no such selling of stock within the overall ratio (unless the Buy/Sell Rules dictate so). It is possible within SSA, that no stock may be sold (according to the Sell Rules), and that the cash is transferred to the bonds-cash portion of the portfolio for years on end. Any stock selling within SSA (and the proceeds transferred to the bond-cash portion) depends on the Sell Rules. The rebalancing within the SSA Strategy occurs only within the individual stock and bond index funds themselves once per year. In the overall view, the stock/bond-cash ratio itself is not rebalanced unless the Sell Rules dictate so. Internal rebalancing within the stock and bond portions of the SSA portfolio simply reestablishes the equal dollar weightings of the individual stock index funds, and the initial listed percentages within the bond-cash portion.

All three of the SSA stock/bond-cash ratio strategies exceeded the returns of the three PR ratios. The final SSA 35/65 stock/bond-cash ratio CAGR exceeded the corresponding PR Ratio CAGR by 39.1%. The final 65/35 SSA stock/bond-cash ratio CAGR exceeded the corresponding CAGR of the PR 65/35 ratio by 33.3%, and the final SSA 50/50 stock/bond-cash ratio CAGR exceeded its PR counterpart by 31.1%.

All in all, the best strategy over 41 years was SSA's 65/35 stock/bond-cash ratio strategy. The worst was the 35/65 PR Strategy. The reason for this large difference in final results for the two strategies, clearly, are the much larger amounts of stock bought at much lower prices, during market crashes, under the SSA Strategy. This had such an effect as to almost triple SSA final nominal and inflation-adjusted dollar returns over the PR dollar returns for their respective 35/65 portfolios.

Let's now look a little more closely at the results of SSA internal rebalancing. In the back-testing process, I was only able to use the S&P 500 index as the purchase mechanism during the buy periods. The SSA Strategy should easily allow an additional one-to-two-percent profit (on average, every two years) over the back-tested results, because of rebalancing within the stock/bond-cash portfolio. There will be index funds within the portfolio that will do worse than others during market crashes and corrections. As those funds are rebalanced within the stock and bond-cash portions, this will provide greater profit without complete rebalancing of the overall stock/bond-cash ratio, as explained earlier, as those lagging funds eventually retrace back up toward pre-crash levels.

Let's say that this additional profit from rebalancing averages one and a half percent every one to two years (the average time that the market stays in bear mode). Or let's say an additional 3 to 4 percent is compounded every 10 years. If a return of 10% to 11% is realized without rebalancing, then this rebalancing effect should result conservatively in at least a 30–35% additional return over an investment lifetime (period of 30–40 years). This, in itself, would represent a very significant additional cash flow during retirement! Plus, this would be accomplished while maintaining fairly large cash and bond balances in the portfolio most of that time, outside of crashes and corrections, reducing overall risk substantially.

During five of the six time periods tested, SSA 65/35 stock/bond-cash ratio returns exceeded those of an All-Stock portfolio (1928–1939, 1972–1988, 1999–2006,

2006–2013, and 1972–2013). The only time period the All-Stock portfolio finished with a higher return was the 1972–1999 period (7.59% CAGR versus 7.46 CAGR, inflation-adjusted). <u>During four time periods (1928–1939, 1972–1988, 1999–2006, and 2006–2013), all three SSA stock/bond-cash ratios returns exceeded</u> those of the All-Stock portfolio. <u>Also, there was not one time period tested, out of all six, in which all three SSA stock/bond-cash ratios tested did not exceed all three PR stock/bond-cash ratios tested in terms of the three measures tested: final overall value (both nominal as well as inflation-adjusted), CR, and CAGR.</u>

You may be wondering why this rebalancing effect does not do more for the PR portfolios. Why is it so often recommended by investment advisers? If rebalancing is so effective, why were the Proportional Rebalancing results so unimpressive? The problem, as explained above, is that PR rebalancing is done every year primarily at the level of the entire stock/bond-cash ratio. This means that every year in which the stock market shows a gain, stock is then sold within the stock portion of the portfolio and moved to the bond-cash portion, thereby limiting future returns as the market continues to advance.

Advisers recommend it, because it has somehow become acceptable to do so. It does reduce risk, and therefore in a market crash, the investor will not lose as much as he or she would if fully invested. As a result, it represents a safer recommendation for investment advisers. They won't be fired as fast. Of course over time, the investor can't match market returns consistently (and probably not even inconsistently).

The Strategic Stock Accumulation Strategy, on the other hand, does no such selling of stock within the overall ratio (unless the Buy/Sell Rules dictate so). No stock may be sold, and cash transferred to the bond/cash portion of the portfolio for years on end. Any stock selling (and proceeds transferred to the bonds-cash portion) depends on the Sell Rules. But when <u>internal rebalancing</u> of the 8 to 10 index funds within the stock portion is added to the strategy, then <u>the results should easily exceed the overall stock market return over an investment lifetime!</u> This is almost impossible to accomplish with the PR or AS strategies. The rebalancing within the SSA Strategy occurs only within each of the stock and bond-cash portions once per year. No funds are transferred from the stock to bond-cash portion or vice versa. This rebalancing simply reestablishes the equal dollar weightings of the individual stock index funds within the stock portion of the portfolio. The **entire** stock/bond-cash rebalancing within SSA takes place as the Sell Rules dictate, and only then.

The most important takeaways from the back-testing were, of course, the final SSA results in comparison to the other two strategies. There is another conclusion that was very clear, which involves the risk associated with all three strategies. The Proportional Rebalancing Strategy can be concluded to have the least overall stock market risk. It always rebalances back to its original cash-bond positions every year in all three ratios. Unfortunately, it is not very successful long-term in comparison to the other two strategies and also to the overall stock market return itself.

Most of the time, stock market returns are quoted in nominal (non-inflation-adjusted) terms. The approximate 10% long-term return of the stock market is often quoted as evidence of the success of stocks in securing one's financial future. The average annual inflation rate, from 1972 to 2013, was 4.29%. This means that the real return over this period, if we accept the 10% figure, was 5.71% (10% minus 4.29%). But here is the most important point: Strategic Stock Accumulation accomplished this, and more, with much less overall risk (and with no internal rebalancing during the back-testing process) than did a 100% All-Stock Strategy!

Most investors simply will not stay with an All-Stock portfolio at all times, because of the severe periodic volatility associated with the stock market. The SSA Strategy catches most, if not all, of the market's return without the periodic stomach-churning effects of an All-Stock portfolio. Yes, the SSA strategy will result in temporary paper losses, as the stock market continues to drop, and you continue to buy. But, unlike the AS strategy, as the stock market retraces back to its previous high and beyond, the SSA investor will have typically bought large amounts of stock at bargain prices. The All-Stock investor would only have gotten 'back to even'. And possibly not back to even after 1 to 2 years of inflation is taken into account.

There are time periods of 10 years or more when the SSA Strategy significantly outperforms the S&P 500. Those results occur just as the stock market retraces back to its previous high by the investor selling, at some point subsequent to the market crash or correction, the stock bought "on sale."

It is unavoidable for SSA to lose some profit potential during times of strong bull markets, because of the larger bond-cash positions built into the strategy. In spite of the fluctuating bond-cash percentages inherent in SSA, the strategy far outperforms the most widely recommended approach by investment managers—Proportional Rebalancing. The bottom line is that SSA allows the investor to capture all of the stock market's return, and more, over time. When internal rebalancing of the 8 to 10 index funds within the stock portion (and 3 in the bond-cash portion) is then added to the strategy, it <u>should easily exceed the overall stock market returns.</u> This is very important for retired investors. It is almost impossible to achieve this with Proportional Rebalancing and an All-Stock Strategy.

Why is the Strategic Stock Accumulation (SSA) Strategy as effective as it has been in comparison to Proportional Rebalancing and the AS-100% All-Stock Strategy during the back-testing process? Not only in terms of actual capital return but also with significantly less risk than the AS Strategy? The obvious answer is <u>volatility</u> and the ability of the strategy to act on it!

When the stock market gets too far ahead of itself, it will eventually conjure up our old friend "reversion to the mean" and begin moving back down in the opposite direction toward fair value, and then past fair value on to undervaluation. Before that occurs, however, stock will typically be sold as per the SSA Sell Rules, and bond and cash index funds would be bought with the proceeds, as the investor's individual stock/bond-cash ratio is reestablished. Then, as the market begins a crash or correction, the investor would start the buying process again thereby increasing the stock portion of the ratio, until selling is again dictated by the Sell Rules.

What John Maynard Keynes, the influential British economist of the early 20th century called "animal spirits" has a lot to do with both stock market "booms" and "busts." Animal spirits can be thought of as "testosterone fueled greed" during stock market booms that lead to a bubble. Then fear occurs during the inevitable subsequent bust and pricking of the bubble. Greed causes investors to "push the envelope" in terms of the debt financing of equity stock purchases. This is coupled with an overconfident sense of personal power as their stock holdings become more and more inflated. This drives stock prices higher and higher as the "greater fool" mindset takes hold.

"Greater fool" refers to the idea that all it takes for a bubble to continue expanding is for sufficient numbers of greater fools to keep buying. Once this pool of naive investors dries up, the end is not far behind. Investors must not only accept but embrace these periodic stock market crashes resulting from fear and greed. They will continue to occur without fail, and investors should not buy like the "greater fool" at market tops but instead buy strategically as the market becomes undervalued during a crash.

The wise investor will wait patiently and be ready to act when the inevitable happens. Not to play defense and protect his assets by selling stock at that time, but to go on the offense, and strategically accumulate stock during the downturn. He will then reap the benefits, as the stock market inevitably retraces its downward path backup to its previous high, and beyond, as the next bull market starts to form. The additional profit gained by rebalancing within the SSA investor's portfolio will allow him or her to beat the return of the overall market. By utilizing the SSA Strategy and following the Pyramid buying pattern of Chart 5, this can be successfully accomplished by any investor.

Looking at Chart 6, we can see that the average stock market decrease through 6 different market crashes was 48.7%. That represents the potential for a lot of profit if the Strategic Stock Accumulation Strategy of Pyramid buying is followed, as outlined in Chart 5. Just remember, when buying stock during this process, you base pyramidal buying levels on downward changes in the S&P 500. However, the actual purchases made, should be allocated in such a way as to rebalance the investor's original stock portfolio percentages (see Charts 1 and 2). As mentioned many times, this will increase your profit as the market retraces back up.

Let's assume, for example, that the S&P 500 is down 23% at year-end, and your chosen SSA stock/bonds-cash ratio (as an older, retired investor) is 35/65. Let's further assume that the investor has $150,000 in the bond-cash portion of his or her portfolio. In that case, the investor would buy stock index funds utilizing 21.4% (Chart 5, Column 6) of his or her bond-cash position, or $32,100. This $32,100 would not be used to buy an S&P 500 index fund, but rather, it would be used to buy the stock index funds in the percentages already predetermined in the stock portion of his chosen Asset Allocation Portfolio. So, if the investor had decided on Chart 1 for asset allocation, then he or she would reestablish those equal stock percentages of 3.5% for each stock index fund (Chart 1, 35/65 stock/bond-cash ratio).

Note that I said, "reestablish," not simply "buy" 3.5% worth of each fund. In other words, if the emerging markets index fund is now down to 2% of the stock portion of the portfolio, then enough of this fund would be bought in order to bring it back up to 3.5%. Likewise, all of the $32,100 is used to purchase additional stock funds in such a way that the resulting stock percentages should equal 3.5% of the total stock portion of the portfolio.

The same procedure would be followed for the bond and cash index fund components of the portfolio. As stock is eventually sold as per the SSA Sell Rules, bond and cash index funds would be bought with the proceeds. In this case, the 35/65 stock/bond-cash ratio would mean that the individual percentages for the bond-cash portion of Chart 1 would be reestablished.

You should now be able to clearly see how these back-tested results solidly support the Strategic Stock Accumulation Strategy. You now have the formula for greater lifetime stock market profit potentials with much less risk! All you need to do is learn and follow it.

Cumulative Return Used in Chart 9

The cumulative return (CR) is the total percentage return of an investment over a specified period of time. It is calculated by subtracting the beginning value from the final value and then dividing this result by the beginning value. It is expressed as follows:

Cumulative Return (CR) =

$$\frac{(\text{Current Price of Security}) - (\text{Original Price of Security})}{(\text{Original Price of Security})}$$

Compound Annual Growth Rate (CAGR) Used in Chart 9

The compound annual growth rate (CAGR) refers to the year-over-year growth rate of an investment through a specified period of time. The compound annual growth rate (CAGR) is calculated by taking the nth root of the total percentage growth rate, where n is the number of years in the period being considered. This can be written as follows:

Compound Annual Growth Rate (CAGR) =

$$CAGR = \left(\frac{\text{Ending Value}}{\text{Beginning Value}}\right)^{\left(\frac{1}{\text{\# of years}}\right)} - 1$$

CHAPTER 10: Some Final Thoughts Before Starting Strategic Stock Accumulation

I would like to end this book by re-emphasizing the importance of making a decision for your financial future. The right decision! Today, investors are bombarded with investment advice from every direction. How can he or she know what to believe or what investment direction to take? With little or no financial education or background, it is easy for beginning investors to become confused. Somewhat surprising, there are experienced investors also who continue to make the same mistakes repeatedly. Why is this so? The main reason, I believe, rests with our old enemies, Fear and Greed (sometimes referred to as "animal spirits"). They both tend to continually overwhelm the most rational minds at the worst possible times.

Strategic Stock Accumulation offers a complete strategy to combat the above perennial emotional market foes. It will, if followed, allow you to control both greed and fear. You will find yourself halfway wishing for a market correction during a roaring bull market (thereby avoiding the worst excesses of greed). Likewise, during a stock market crash, you, hopefully will be buying "joyously" with little fear or sleepless nights. This, the result of a simple but complete, methodical strategy that allows primarily the emotion of satisfaction, borne of confidence in a system that you can easily understand.

As you begin to implement SSA, there are several stock market principles regarding your portfolio that are important for investors to remember: First, to turn former President Franklin D. Roosevelt's famous admonition on its head, I would argue: "The thing we need to fear is over-confidence itself," especially as it regards investing in the stock market. Does that really sound right? Didn't I say confidence in SSA should be a normal byproduct of the system? That is true. But, a healthy respect (not overconfidence borne of pride) for the stock market, based on the confidence one has to follow his/her system's strategy and not succumb to greed as the stock market continues to make new highs, is good.

In Adam Smith's (his pseudonym) popular book of the 1960s, "The Money Game," he talks about one investment company that always preferred younger men to actually do the buying and selling in stock. Why? Because under a certain age, investors, including investment managers and traders, have no memory or experience of any severe stock market crashes. They are therefore willing to take far more chances and "push the envelope" in order to gain short-term profits. Unfortunately, as I explained earlier, short-term profits are the name of the game for many managed mutual funds. The longer term is a different story.

The problem is those regular, nasty stock market crashes. Those financial shocks to a manager's confidence, as well as to individual investors' confidence, eventually causes most of these guys and gals to get religion. But it takes one, and sometimes two, market crashes to accomplish this. And even then, some managers and individuals investors never "get it."

Some continue to be victims of another psychological market condition called "survivor bias," (as well as having "recency" issues, as discussed earlier). Survivor bias is that mental state that some investors who have "survived" the last market crash fall into. "Okay, so the market dropped 60% five years ago. I'm still here, I'm back up again, and the market is on to new heights. I'm not going to miss any of this upward movement in the stock market. Besides, this time it's different (five very dangerous words). The stock market is on firmer footing than it was during the last market crash. And, this time, I'll know when to get out before it's too late."

If this investor held on and did not sell any stock

during the last crash, then yes, he survived okay (assuming he was not older and/or retired), as the market subsequently retraced, but many investors panic as the market goes down, and then sell most, if not all, of their stock. Then they either swear off the market completely, or they get back into the market long after it has started its retracing process back up. The commonplace thinking usually is as follows: "I guess it's safe now to get back in; everyone else is in and making money again."

Instead of getting back to even, when the market returns to its previous high, these investors are locked into a loss at that point, because they sold their stock on the way down and cannot benefit from the move back up. Even the investor who stayed the course with a fully invested 100% All-Stock portfolio and eventually got back to even had risked a large part of his portfolio needlessly. This could have been catastrophic if he was retired and the market just happened to stay down longer than he could wait. Maybe he depended on the income from his portfolio for living expenses and was forced to sell part of his stock, regardless, in a declining market. So, avoid survivor bias, as just explained. On the other hand, if we choose to define survivor bias as a learning experience gained from the last crash, and we use this experience to act rationally during the next crash, then the term has positive meaning.

Remember to always keep a substantial percentage of your portfolio in bonds-cash (as determined by SSA), and don't sell as the stock market goes down—instead, buy! This must mean that you have money to buy stock with. And this can only occur if your portfolio always includes sufficient cash and/or bonds before a crash or correction begins.

The above discussion of survivor bias and stock market crashes begs the questions: "What causes these crashes?" and "Why can't the stock market just continue on a nice smooth, maybe even slower, upward trajectory, as it simply reflects overall corporate profits on an annual basis?" Well, as explained previously, in a free-market capitalist economy like ours, it just doesn't work that way. It is human nature to overreact to investment opportunities in different parts of the economy, whether it's real estate, construction, mortgage lending, commodity speculation, or the stock market. Too much money is eventually borrowed to finance some or all of the above areas of the economy, and the returns on those investments, at some point, can't cover the interest payments. Then, the bubble that developed from all the greed, speculation, and borrowed money, bursts. Bankruptcies (and/or expensive bailouts) are the result. Most of the debt is eventually cleared, and the process starts all over again.

This doesn't really sound like a good system, does it? But, it is. It is actually better than any other economic system ever devised by man. This is because, as a result of the aftermath of the booms and bubbles, corrections and crashes, most people living in free-market capitalist economy actually experience a higher standard of living over time. The primary reason for this is the continued advances made in technology that are vigorously promoted by free-market capitalism, based on risk. Most of the world's inventions and technological improvements over the last 100 years originated in the United States by men and women (not only investors) willing to take on risk.

Okay, so as investors following the SSA Strategy, we don't need to worry about periodic stock market crashes. Is there anything we do need to worry about that hasn't been mentioned? Well, we shouldn't really worry about the ones I'm about to mention, because there's nothing we can do about most of them anyway. These are the rare occurrences that no one can predict and that are referred to as "black swan" events (or "tail risk"). In a capitalist democracy like ours, with a strong military and infrastructure, the worst results of these events are minimized (but are less likely to be minimized in emerging market countries).

What are examples of these events? World war, sudden and unprepared for, is one. Pearl Harbor was an example, although that particular black swan event led to the U.S. entry into World War II, which, ironically in the longer term, helped lead the U.S. out of the Great Depression. This was because the huge labor and manufacturing requirements of that war stimulated the economy big-time. Most black swan events don't have that result, at least on a short-term basis. There was a short-term stock market drop after the Pearl Harbor attack, as well as the "9/11" attack on the Twin Towers. After both of these attacks, the market rebounded.

Sudden war can be catastrophic, economically, for a smaller country unable to adapt to it. Severe earthquakes, tsunamis, hurricanes, and tornadoes are other examples that can be very hard on emerging market economies and their stock markets. Imagine how a super volcano or very large asteroid crashing anywhere would affect all life on earth, not to mention the world economy. Other possibilities are the loss of human technological control to silicon-based super-computer intelligence. This will become much more of a threat as nations continue to relinquish more and more control to "the machines" in a naive (after a certain point) attempt to make our lives easier.

The point at which super-computer intelligence becomes self-aware is not far away. Controlling this threat will be a real challenge in the near future. As Stephen Hawking, the world's most famous living physicist says, artificial intelligence (AI) could be our "worst mistake in history." Hawking is not alone in projecting this possible dismal future. He, as well as other physicists, voice increasing concern about the superiority of super advanced technological intelligence one day competing with us, instead of helping us. To believe we can continue to take advantage of such technology, ever increasing in intelligence and self-awareness, for our own utility, is to simply go into denial about the problem. That's not to say we are incapable of finding ways to control it, only that it will become increasingly difficult to do so.

I've already mentioned the threat of a nuclear bomb (or dirty bomb) exploding somewhere in the developed world on purpose or by accident. There is also the threat of other weapons of mass destruction being unleashed, such as those chemical or biological. Imagine what any of these possibilities coming to fruition on a large scale would do to the stock markets around the world. The S&P 500 corporations, as I have said, do at least 30% of their business in

Europe, and more and more U.S. companies are increasingly engaged in business with emerging market countries. The world is now very interdependent economically, and regarding some of these black swan events, many individual countries can easily fall, as well as rise, together.

Probably the biggest challenge facing a stock market investor is another one that he or she has no control over. This challenge involves no black swan event. The challenge that I now refer to is more psychological. It is the mental difficulty of dealing with the occasional long periods of time (for example, between 1900 and 1920) when the stock market makes little or no progress at all in terms of annual closing values. This situation is different from dealing with a stock market crash. On January 2, 1901, the Dow closed at 70.44. On December 31, 1920 (20 years later), the Dow closed at 71.95. That's a gain of just 1.51% over 20 years! But, eight years later, after the so-called "roaring twenties" and at the market's high point of 1929 (just before the start of the crash of 1929), it closed almost five times higher! On January 2, 1929 the Dow closed at 307.01. It wasn't until the January 2, 1953 year-end that it closed close to this figure. However, as mentioned earlier, because of deflation and dividends, a buy-and-hold investor would have been made whole (back to even) about four and a half years after the crash of 1929. On December 31, 1965 the Dow closed at 969.6. On December 31, 1981 the dollar was still at 875. This was 16 years later, and the market still finished below the close of 1965.

The first example I gave starting in 1901 shows the Dow lingering for 20 years, without any advance, and in the second example, beginning in 1929, this stock market "malaise" had lasted 24 years! Having painted this dismal picture, why would anyone ever want to take a chance on the stock market? What if this happens again? Don't these historical facts show just how risky the stock market can be for a long-term investor? And if not risky, at least a waste of time?

The answers are as follows: 1) The stock market can be very profitable. 2) The stock market will have times of "no growth." 3) Yes, it can be risky. But this risk is what allows for greater profits in the stock market. 4) The stock market is not a waste of time. Let's look at these answers a little closer. An investor must accept greater risk for a greater return on any investment. This is 'Investment 101.' The best time to buy is when the market looks the riskiest. As Baron Von Rothschild, the 17th century British banker, said: "Buy, when the blood is running in the streets," and Warren Buffet says: "I like to buy when others are selling, and sell when others are buying." Also, keep in mind that it is much less risky to own index funds than individual stocks, as explained in the chapter devoted to them. There is also the risk of "opportunity costs." These are the costs of staying invested in a trendless stock market and losing the opportunity of possibly earning a higher return in some other more profitable investment.

Risk, however, can be controlled, with the effective use of asset allocation and diversification. The stock market never has to be a waste of time. And, here is the best news about a "trendless" stock market, especially for the SSA investor. Even during those long periods of time when the stock market appears to make no progress, it is through the normal volatility of quickly changing prices that investors are able to take advantage of the drops in the market in order to buy stock and then hold it, as the stock market typically then makes a 20 to a 50% retracing move back upward. Remember this!

These opportunities occur even within those long periods of time when few or no new lasting stock market highs are achieved. For example, in the middle of the Great Depression, in 1932, the stock market (the Dow) closed on July 8 at 41.32, and on January 2, 1934, it closed at 100.36. That's an upward move in the stock market of 143% in a year and a half—in the middle of the worst depression in U.S. history! On December 31, 1903, the Dow closed at 49. On the night of January 2, 1906, it closed at 95—an increase of 93% in 2 years. And on January 2, 1975, the Dow closed at 632.04. On December 31, 1976, it closed at 1004.65—a stock market gain of 84% in 2 years. In each of these three cases, the low stock market levels I cited were succeeded by significantly higher year-end stock market prices in the next one to four years. And within the SSA system, that is when we buy - year-end! Those were the times when SSA could have been very profitably put to use, by buying those stocks on sale at the time. As the stock market dropped, the investor could have used the Pyramid buying method of SSA, held the stock bought, and then profited, as the market retraced back up closer to its fair value levels.

Stocks have not historically been the only profitable part of an investor's portfolio. You may wonder at the lost profit potential of the older retired investor who conservatively maintains a 65% bond-cash position in his portfolio (and only 35% in stock). Today, as of July 2014, that cash is earning almost nothing, with money market rates near zero. But historically, the cumulative average of the U.S. prime interest rate from 1947 to the present is 9.84% (very good for bonds)! The U.S. all-time high prime rate was 21.5% on December 19, 1980 through January 2, 1981.

Historically, cash (money market funds) and bonds of different durations, have significantly contributed to overall portfolio returns. It is best to invest in bonds of shorter maturities, however when involved with the SSA Strategy, because this reduces the duration (time) risk associated with rising interest rates. This allows an investor to switch to cash from bonds more quickly when necessary, without worrying about a significant capital loss. So, in addition to the profit potential of utilizing SSA during those periods of stock market drift, by taking advantage of the buying opportunities resulting from year-end short-term volatility, bonds can also contribute to the portfolio. Even during those periodic episodes when the stock market goes nowhere, large cash and bond positions usually (but not always) contribute to returns. Don't forget, the bond-cash portion of the portfolio is also internally rebalanced at year-end.

It is important to emphasize once more the absolute necessity of not being 100% fully invested in the stock market after the age of 55. Of course, some of the worst Armageddon-like, black swan possibilities would render useless any stock market strategy, at any age. If the central record-keeping and control areas of Fidelity or Vanguard and all electronic communication is destroyed or severely compromised, it won't matter how much you have in cash and stock at those brokerages. At that point, a whole different set of survival skills would be necessary.

However, on a much more positive note, most black swan events would not lead to Armageddon but rather something much better for the SSA investor. As I've emphasized many times up until now, for those with cash available, the temporary drop in the stock market can leave large parts of it "on sale" until the majority of investors realize that a particular event is not the end of the world. The reaction of the stock market to 9/11 provides a good example. Within several weeks after that terrorist attack, the stock market had retraced the sudden drop resulting from it, and some wise investors profited again.

Why do I talk about any of these black swan events at all, if the chance is very small that any of the worst ones will occur, and if there's nothing we can do about it anyway? Maybe I shouldn't have, but it is always a good idea to look ahead in life, and try to anticipate a possible "worst-case scenario" when implementing SSA Strategy.

The conclusion I've come to, in the case of the different black swan possibilities, is not to let them change my actions one iota, except to take advantage of them financially in the stock market! I hope the very small risk of an extreme black swan event doesn't discourage you from investing in the stock market. Maybe you weren't even considering them as a possibility at all until I brought it up. Sorry! Regardless, we can't base any of our important life decisions on the possibility that one "might" occur. After all, if we did, who would ever have children, for example, fearing what they "might" have to endure? We cannot let these very small risks paralyze our actions. I was advised by some not to even talk about these "negative possibilities." But, why not?

Most successful investors are mature adults, with an independent nature, who make their own decisions based on all the information that they can get. I can't believe that discussing the above subject will dissuade anyone of them from making money with SSA, or attempting any invest-ment strategy, for that matter. Plus, if you look at these rare occurrences as opportunities, rather than thinking that "the world going to hell in a handbasket," then it is worth discussing.

I want to leave you with one final thought. The ancient Romans had advice that they were said to live by: "Carpe Diem," which means "Seize the Day!" in Latin. Learn the strategy of Strategic Stock Accumulation. Use it. Let it work for you, so that you will be able to financially 'Seize the Day,' resulting with your success in the stock market.

Now you have all the information that you need to start making money from the next stock market correction or crash—or even just profit from the normal volatility that regularly occurs in the stock market. All you require at this point is the 'vision' to see your future unfolding as it should. Laser focus with the confidence that you now have to follow through, secure in the knowledge that Strategic Stock Accumulation will work for your financial future. I hope that you will take the first step toward less stress and more profitable investing by embracing SSA as a total port-folio strategy. If you follow it, without deviating, you will be well on your way toward financial independence.

Addendum

The information in this addendum was originally on my website only, stephenrperry.com. After thinking more about this, I decided it was important to have these graph charts available within the E-Book. A careful perusal of these graphs show clearly and much more dramatically the results of the back-testing I personally did, in which the three different stock and bond investment strategies were tested over six different time periods. Though research has not been my profession, I will let the reader judge the accuracy of these charts and their accompanying tables. I have spent literally hundreds of hours checking and rechecking the figures. The actual sixteen column tables documenting all the numbers comprising these graphs are all on my website. They were simply too large to include in this E-Book, and the numbers on these tables would have ended up too small to be clearly viewable. On the website, http://www.stephenrperry.com, however, they are easily viewable.

One final point: If you have any questions whatsoever about this book or how to implement the SSA 'Buy' and 'Sell' Rules, please go to my website and hit the 'contact' button and ask your question(s). I'll get back to you by email, probably within 24 hours. Finally, a password is no longer required to access all Graphs and Tables on the website.

Strategic Stock Accumulation (SSA) Documentation

Six Time Periods Graphs/Tables
Graphs and Corresponding Tables:

2006-2013 I   *(A,B,C,D,E,F,G)**
1999-2006 II   (A,B,C,D,E,F,G)
1972-1988 III   (A,B,C,D,E,F,G)
1928-1939 IV   (A,B,C,D,E,F,G)
1988-1999 V   (A,B,C,D,E,F,G)
    1988 figures cumulative back to 1972
1999-2013 VI   (A,B,C,D,E,F,G)
    1999 figures cumulative back to 1972

Roman numerals represent Graphs
**Letters represent Tables corresponding to Graphs*

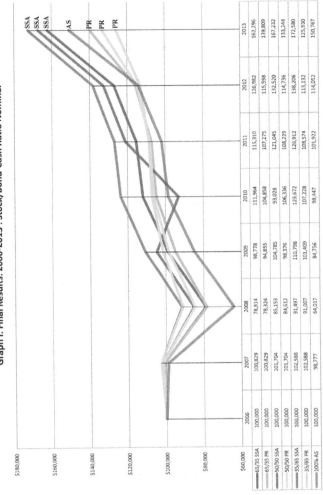

Graph I: Final Results: 2006-2013 : Stock/bond-Cash Ratio Nominal

	2006	2007	2008	2009	2010	2011	2012	2013
65/35 SSA	100,000	100,829	78,814	98,778	111,964	115,310	126,982	162,296
65/35 PR	100,000	100,829	78,324	94,855	104,858	107,275	115,598	139,809
50/50 SSA	100,000	101,704	85,153	104,785	93,028	121,045	132,520	167,232
50/50 PR	100,000	101,704	84,612	98,376	106,336	108,229	114,736	133,244
35/65 SSA	100,000	102,588	91,497	110,798	123,672	126,912	138,206	172,580
35/65 PR	100,000	102,588	91,007	101,409	107,228	108,574	113,132	125,930
100% AS	100,000	98,777	64,017	84,756	98,447	101,922	114,052	150,767

SSA: Strategic Stock Accumulation   PR: Proportional Rebalancing   AS: All Stock Portfolio

Strategic Stock Accumulation Strategy, SSA (all three top lines-maroon shades), outperformed both Proportional Rebalancing, PR (all three green shades) and the All-Stock, AS, (blue shade) at all three Stock/bond-Cash ratios (65/35, 50/50, and 35/65) by testing endpoint 2013, year-end.

The 50/50 SSA Stock/Bond-Cash ratio briefly drops below the other two strategies during part of 2009-2010, as large amounts of crash-driven stock purchases took place. By mid-2010, however, the large amount of stock bought "on sale", drove the strategy above both of the other two. For example, by 2013 the 35/65 SSA Strategy outperformed the 35/65 PR Strategy by 37%.

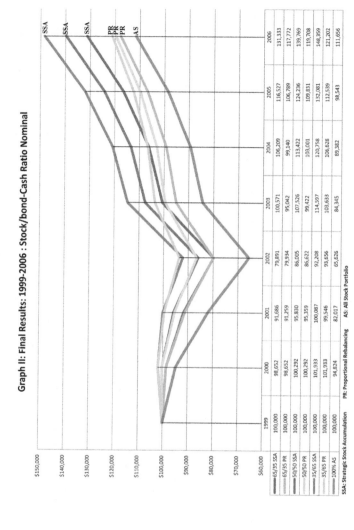

Graph II: Final Results: 1999-2006 : Stock/bond-Cash Ratio Nominal

	1999	2000	2001	2002	2003	2004	2005	2006
65/35 SSA	100,000	98,652	91,686	79,891	100,571	106,209	116,527	131,333
65/35 PR	100,000	98,652	91,259	79,934	95,042	99,140	106,789	117,772
50/50 SSA	100,000	100,292	95,830	86,005	107,526	113,422	124,236	139,769
50/50 PR	100,000	100,292	95,359	86,622	99,422	103,001	109,831	119,708
35/65 SSA	100,000	101,933	100,087	92,208	114,597	120,758	132,081	148,359
35/65 PR	100,000	101,933	99,546	93,656	103,633	106,628	112,539	121,202
100% AS	100,000	94,824	82,017	65,626	84,345	89,382	98,543	111,656

SSA: Strategic Stock Accumulation   PR: Proportional Rebalancing   AS: All Stock Portfolio

The Proportional Rebalancing Strategy (PR) keeps pace with the Strategic Stock Accumulation Strategy, at all three Stock/ Bond-Cash ratios until 2003-2004, as the crash-driven SSA Strategy stock purchases of all three SSA portfolios begin to benefit from the stock market retracing back up to and beyond pre-crash levels. By the end of 2004, all three SSA portfolio ratios pull ahead of all other strategies at all three ratios. The 35/65 SSA Strategy outperformed the corresponding 35/65 PR Strategy by 27.2%; the 65/35 SSA Strategy outperformed the 65/35 PR Strategy by 11.5% (cumulative returns)

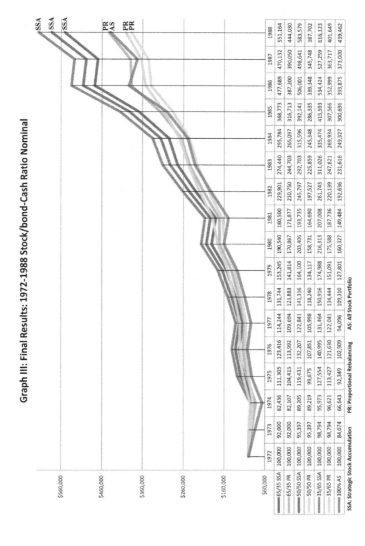

Graph III: Final Results: 1972-1988 Stock/bond-Cash Ratio Nominal

	1972	1973	1974	1975	1976	1977	1978	1979	1980	1981	1982	1983	1984	1985	1986	1987	1988
65/35 SSA	100,000	92,000	82,436	111,305	123,416	114,244	131,744	153,245	190,540	180,500	229,901	274,440	295,784	368,773	477,689	470,132	551,164
65/35 PR	100,000	92,000	82,107	104,415	113,992	109,694	123,883	141,814	170,867	171,877	210,750	244,703	265,097	316,713	387,200	390,050	444,030
50/50 SSA	100,000	95,397	89,205	119,431	132,207	122,841	141,316	164,100	203,406	193,735	245,797	292,703	315,596	392,141	506,001	498,641	583,579
50/50 PR	100,000	95,397	89,219	99,675	107,851	105,998	118,240	134,117	158,731	164,690	197,527	225,859	245,348	286,335	339,348	345,748	387,702
35/65 SSA	100,000	98,794	95,973	127,554	140,995	131,464	150,916	174,988	216,313	207,008	261,743	311,026	335,474	415,593	534,424	527,259	616,123
35/65 PR	100,000	98,794	96,621	113,427	121,630	122,041	134,444	151,091	175,588	187,736	220,139	247,821	269,934	307,566	352,999	363,717	401,649
100% AS	100,000	84,074	66,643	92,349	102,909	94,096	109,310	127,801	160,327	149,484	192,636	231,616	249,327	300,696	393,875	373,000	439,462

SSA: Strategic Stock Accumulation   PR: Proportional Rebalancing   AS: All Stock Portfolio

Because of stock market crash/corrections, stock was bought as per the Buy Rules of the SSA Strategy in '73, '74, and '81. This allowed the SSA Strategy to significantly outperform the other two back-tested strategies actually by 1982, and much more significantly, by 1988, year-end.

For example, the 50/50 SSA strategy outperformed the 50/50 PR Strategy by 50.5%; the 35/65 SSA Strategy exceeded the 35/65 PR return by 53.4%. The SSA Strategy out returned the AS Strategy at all three SSA ratios over this total time period.

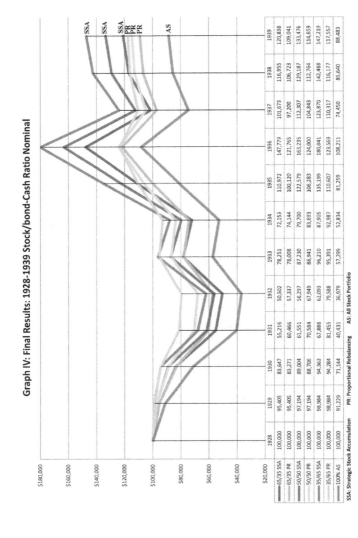

Graph IV: Final Results: 1928-1939 Stock/bond-Cash Ratio Nominal

	1928	1929	1930	1931	1932	1933	1934	1935	1936	1937	1938	1939
65/35 SSA	100,000	95,405	83,647	55,216	50,502	78,251	72,153	110,972	147,779	101,673	116,955	120,838
65/35 PR	100,000	95,405	83,271	60,466	57,337	78,008	74,144	100,120	121,765	97,200	106,723	109,041
50/50 SSA	100,000	97,194	89,004	61,551	56,297	87,230	79,700	122,579	163,235	112,307	129,187	133,476
50/50 PR	100,000	97,194	88,706	70,584	67,949	86,941	83,693	106,283	124,000	104,843	112,764	114,659
35/65 SSA	100,000	98,984	94,363	67,888	62,093	96,210	87,905	135,199	180,041	123,870	142,488	147,219
35/65 PR	100,000	98,984	94,284	81,455	79,588	95,391	92,987	110,607	123,569	110,317	116,177	117,557
100% AS	100,000	91,229	71,144	40,431	36,979	57,299	52,834	81,259	108,211	74,450	85,640	88,483

SSA: Strategic Stock Accumulation   PR: Proportional Rebalancing   AS: All Stock Portfolio

All of the Bond-Cash portion of all three SSA ratio strategies was used up buying stock in 1929, 1930, and 1931. By mid-1936, these earlier crash related stock purchases allowed all three SSA Strategies to forge ahead of the other two strategies, so that at the 35/65, 50/50, and 65/35 SSA ratio strategies they each exceeded the PR corresponding returns by 25.2%, 16.4%, and 10.8%. SSA 35/65 ratio strategy outperformed the All-Stock, (AS) Strategy by 66.4% during this time period, showing more clearly how a severe stock market crash (like the "Great Depression") can devastate an All-Stock portfolio for a long period of time.

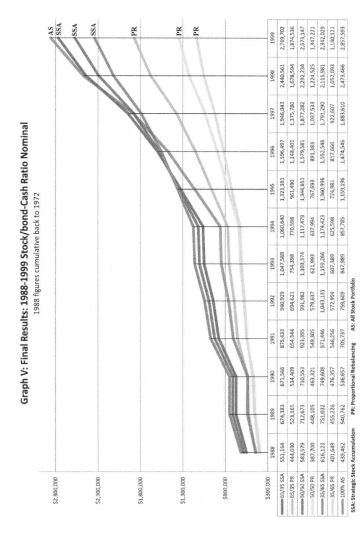

Graph V: Final Results: 1988-1999 Stock/bond-Cash Ratio Nominal

1988 figures cumulative back to 1972

	1988	1989	1990	1991	1992	1993	1994	1995	1996	1997	1998	1999
65/35 SSA	551,164	674,383	671,566	875,433	940,929	1,047,588	1,060,640	1,323,381	1,596,497	1,946,043	2,440,561	2,769,702
65/35 PR	444,030	523,165	534,409	654,344	694,621	754,398	770,598	961,490	1,148,401	1,375,780	1,678,594	1,874,536
50/50 SSA	583,579	712,673	710,553	923,395	991,982	1,103,374	1,117,479	1,344,651	1,579,581	1,877,282	2,292,234	2,573,147
50/50 PR	387,700	448,105	463,321	549,305	579,637	621,993	637,994	767,693	891,383	1,037,533	1,224,525	1,347,221
35/65 SSA	616,123	751,032	749,608	971,446	1,043,131	1,159,266	1,174,423	1,360,956	1,552,548	1,791,290	2,115,981	2,342,029
35/65 PR	401,649	455,226	476,357	546,256	572,959	607,389	625,598	724,981	817,666	922,607	1,052,093	1,140,121
100% AS	439,462	540,762	536,657	705,737	759,609	847,989	857,785	1,159,196	1,474,546	1,883,610	2,473,466	2,857,593

SSA: Strategic Stock Accumulation   PR: Proportional Rebalancing   AS: All Stock Portfolio

The years between 1994 and 1999 were fantastic for an All-Stock portfolio, as there were no market crashes or corrections, showing the power of an All-Stock portfolio during such a strong uninterrupted bull run. The SSA (Strategic Stock Accumulation) 65/35 portfolio however, kept pace very well, in spite of its contrary power as a bear market strategy, being exceeded by AS by only 1.7%. SSA outperformed PR at the 65/35, 50/50, and 35/65 ratios by an astounding 47.8%, 91%, and 105.4% at the corresponding PR ratios.

Graph VI: Final Results: 1999-2013 Stock/bond-Cash Ratio Nominal
1999 figures cumulative back to 1972

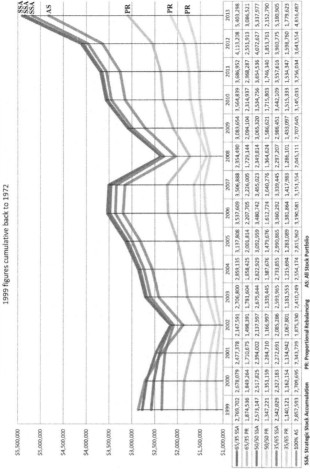

	1999	2000	2001	2002	2003	2004	2005	2006	2007	2008	2009	2010	2011	2012	2013
65/35 SSA	2,769,702	2,678,079	2,477,378	2,147,591	2,706,800	2,859,135	3,137,808	3,537,609	3,506,888	2,354,490	3,083,654	3,564,839	3,686,952	4,113,208	5,403,298
65/35 PR	1,874,536	1,849,264	1,710,675	1,498,391	1,781,604	1,858,425	2,001,814	2,207,705	2,226,005	1,729,144	2,094,104	2,314,937	2,368,287	2,551,913	3,086,521
50/50 SSA	2,573,147	2,517,825	2,394,002	2,137,597	2,675,644	2,822,929	3,092,559	3,480,742	3,455,023	2,349,814	3,065,320	3,534,756	3,654,536	4,072,627	5,337,977
50/50 PR	1,347,221	1,351,159	1,284,710	1,166,997	1,339,445	1,387,676	1,479,676	1,612,724	1,640,276	1,364,624	1,586,621	1,715,803	1,746,340	1,853,761	2,152,790
35/65 SSA	2,342,029	2,327,183	2,272,691	2,085,286	2,593,965	2,733,855	2,990,865	3,360,292	3,339,445	2,297,207	2,986,451	3,442,109	3,557,616	3,960,775	5,180,905
35/65 PR	1,140,121	1,162,154	1,134,942	1,067,801	1,181,553	1,215,694	1,283,089	1,381,864	1,417,983	1,286,101	1,433,097	1,515,333	1,534,347	1,598,750	1,779,623
100% AS	2,857,593	2,709,695	2,343,729	1,875,330	2,410,249	2,554,174	2,815,962	3,190,581	3,151,554	2,045,111	2,707,645	3,145,033	3,256,034	3,643,554	4,816,487

SSA: Strategic Stock Accumulation   PR: Proportional Rebalancing   AS: All Stock Portfolio

The beginning 1999 totals for all three strategies are cumulative back to 1972. As is apparent from those beginning numbers, there were already large differences up to that point, between the PR Strategy, and the other two back-tested strategies, SSA and AS, the PR Strategy lagging significantly. The final 2013 results show the superiority of the Strategic Stock Accumulation Strategy, SSA, (three maroon shades), over the All-Stock Strategy, AS (blue shade), and the Proprtional Rebalancing Strategy, PR, (three green shades).

All three SSA ratio Strategies outperformed all four other ratio strategies (three PR and one AS). The 65/35 SSA (Strategic Stock Accumulation) Strategy outperformed the AS, All-Stock Strategy by 12.2% with much lower risk over the entire 41 year period. As the graph shows, the average of the three SSA Strategies exceeded the PR returns over this 41 year period by approximately 114%. This fact alone should give a long-term investor serious pause before considering Proportional Rebalancing as a long-term strategy.

Made in the USA
Middletown, DE
03 February 2020